STALIN'S WAR

STALIN'S WAR

A Radical New Theory of the Origins of the
Second World War

Ernst Topitsch

Translated by
A. and B.E. Taylor

St. Martin's Press
New York

First published in the United States of America in 1987

Library of Congress Cataloging-in-Publication Data

Topitsch, Ernst, 1919-
  Stalin's war

  Translation of: Stalin's Kreig
  Bibliography: p.
  Includes index.
  1. World War, 1939-1945—Diplomatic history.
2. Soviet Union—Foreign relations—1917-1945.
3. Communist Strategy. I. Title
D754.S5T6713   1987   940.53′2   87-16332
ISBN 0-312-00989-5

Typeset in Clearface by Rapidset & Design, London WC1
Printed and bound in Great Britain by
Richard Clay (The Chaucer Press) Ltd, Bungay, Suffolk

Contents

Preface

The present work ventures, looking back over forty years, to contribute new and significant insights into our political understanding of the Second World War and to offer a more comprehensive overview of the sequence and interplay of events in this, the greatest catastrophe of the present century. Such a venture involves important changes in perspective: Hitler and Nazi Germany forfeit their position at the centre of the stage and make only episodic appearances – chess pieces rather than players – forming part of a long-term strategy already conceived by Lenin which aimed at the subjection of the 'capitalist' world. The full significance of Stalin's role in the realisation of this grandiose conception has not been fully grasped by the historical research so far undertaken. Even in Soviet Russia, during the 'de-Stalinisation' which followed the 'personality cult', the part played by the demonic Georgian in the rise of his country to superpower status is frequently and unjustifiably disparaged. However, as the events in question recede in time it becomes much clearer that Stalin is an outstanding figure, not merely in Russian history, like Peter the Great or Ivan the Terrible, but also in world history.

Particular emphasis must be laid on the cunning and finesse displayed by the red czar in executing that long-term strategy, and on the tactics he employed, neither of which have so far received the appreciation they deserve. The basic premises on which these tactics are based have proved enduringly efficient and should be carefully considered, especially by future generations. Not without reason does Mephistopheles, in Goethe's *Faust*, say to the 'younger members in the pit, who don't applaud':

> Cold you remain at words from me,
> For you young children, I'll let it be:
> Consider, the Devil's an old hand,
> Get old yourselves, you'll understand!

I should like to thank all those who have helped me with the composition and publication of the book, in particular my assistant, Dr Peter Payer, who helped me in the procurement of relevant literature, not always an easy task, and my secretary, Mrs Gudrun Reime.

I must also express my thanks to two historians for their encouragement: Professor Werner Conze, my former Heidelberg colleague, and Dr Wilhelm Ritter von Schramm, who through his book *Speak of Peace If You Want War* considerably helped my understanding of psychological warfare. Unfortunately, Dr von Schramm passed away before I could consult him about the plan of this work. What follows I gratefully dedicate to his memory, in the conviction that the reflections developed here would have met with his approval.

Ernst Topitsch, Graz, January 1985

Introduction

This work is the result of studies made at various times over a considerable period. They were undertaken first and foremost for private reasons: as the work progressed, however, what was intended originally merely for purposes of self-clarification began to yield results which varied considerably from current conceptions, and for this reason they demanded publication.

A few personal details may be worth mentioning: I belonged to one of the divisions which, following the Western Campaign of 1940, was sent from France to Poland, into the area of the Demarcation Line. There I lived through those fateful months when the hopes for peace of the early summer dwindled away, to be replaced by a gnawing worry that the real war was now about to start. The soldier in the ranks had, of course, no insight into the policy and strategy of his superiors; but my deductions from the censored news at home and occasional information from abroad yielded more and more the impression that, in spite of victories already won, Germany had reached a dead end. England was not yet defeated, American hostility was growing, and behind the Demarcation Line the Russian sphinx was lying in wait. Then, on 22 June 1941, the die was cast. The division to which I belonged perished in Stalingrad, a fate which I myself escaped only by a stroke of good fortune.

During these months of gnawing uncertainty I felt the urge to clarify my thoughts concerning the cause and background of these happenings to which I had to submit in ignorance. Yet even in those depressing times a kind of mentor was standing at my side, in the form of the great Greek historian Thucydides, who witnessed the mutual carnage of the Hellenes in the Peloponnesian Wars. The truths told in his histories offer a message of uncomfortable accuracy for the present day. I went – with Thucydides, as it were, in my knapsack – through a war which had an impact on Europe every bit as calamitous as the wars of ancient Greece. The eternal quality of Thucydides' work is, however,

1

less due to his treatment of events in Greece more than two thousand years ago than to his insight into political thinking. The great speeches, in which the historian invites the actors to unfold their motives and intentions with absolute clarity, are model lessons in the operation of that catch-all justification so beloved of all politicians of all periods, 'reasons of state', and are infinitely superior to the later literature on the subject. All his expositions have a sober and caustic tone, by which the sum of the experiences and sufferings of the time is crystallised into knowledge and understanding. It can be seen, therefore, that even during the war I was deeply involved in historical and political thinking, a field in which my interest was quickened by my work in social philosophy and the social sciences. I am, admittedly, not a historian, nor can I offer any new documents in support of the theories proposed; but just as it is the observer who sees most of the game, so widely-known documents may reveal to the outsider surprising connections which may hitherto have been overlooked; solutions may be found to problems which have been blocking the path of research for some considerable time. It must also be admitted that this present work owes much to other authors, especially Grigore Gafencu, George F. Kennan, Philipp W. Fabry and Andreas Hillgruber, as also to the investigations into the field of military science by the former colonel of the General Staff, Erich Helmdach.

This present work is not simply concerned with portraying and analysing those unique events which are concentrated in the two years or so between the Hitler–Stalin pact and the attack on the Soviet Union; nor is it solely concerned with fitting these events into a more comprehensive historical framework, though it does also attempt to do this. The intention is to offer an insight into the structure and methods of sophisticated power politics. This seems of special importance since in the aftermath of the excesses of National Socialism and its military consequences, the relationship of the German people to this undoubtedly difficult and often terrifying passage in their history has some distinctly disturbing features. But the 'demonry of power' – to mention the title of Gerhard Ritter's outstanding work, now unfortunately seldom read – cannot be got rid of simply by closing one's eyes to it. On the contrary, those who don't believe in the demonic influence of power will, with deadly certainty, fall victim to it.

Such demons are not easily exorcised, though many people who are well-meaning but politically inexperienced or simply young appear to believe that they are. On the contrary, the will to power is a fundamental element of our existence, with its origins in the animals from which we evolved. The latest research studies propose that the intelligence of the *hominidae*, and so of human beings, was developed first in struggles for leadership and power within the group, and was only subsequently applied to more practical purposes. Thus behaviour orientated towards a desired end in the social sphere – often referred to as 'the social use of tools' – would precede the technical use of tools in the history of the tribe.[1] This would begin to explain how the technologically backward civilisations of ancient India and China produced refined political doctrines such as the Arthashastra of Kautilya or the writings of Sun-tse, which still have validity – in their first principles – in the era of space travel and atomic power. There are, indeed, numerous political practices which are old and well tried, especially the trick, the very embodiment of the 'social use of tools', of getting one's intentions carried out by others, if possible without their noticing it. By so doing, the user of this artifice can keep himself in the background and usually achieve his aims with a minimum of expense or risk.

Yet such actions are morally problematical. Kant's highest ethical principle, unequivocally stated, was that a fellow human being must always be considered as an end, not merely as a means. Thucydides also reflected on the possibilities for conflict between politics and ethics – possibilities which Christianity has exacerbated without offering any solutions in return. Max Weber made many pointed remarks on this theme in his classic lecture 'Politics as a Profession'. There are various ways of trying to overcome these difficulties. By calling on morally noble ends, which may be real or assumed, one can try to justify the morally questionable or objectionable means which are allegedly or actually necessary for the achievement of those ends. Warriors of all creeds and in every century, fighting for their gods or their religious beliefs, have excused their deeds with this justification. It is, however, more than obvious that noble ends are often no more than a pretext to justify or conceal quite different intentions.[2] On the other hand, this stance may equally be taken out of genuinely good intentions, with the instigator either unaware of the problem lurking here or failing to give it due weight. Unfortunately, a pragmatic attitude which seeks to avoid both these morally dubious avenues is frequently misunderstood, and it is because of this that Machiavelli had to pay for his frankness with centuries of defamation. Also noteworthy here is Gerhard Ritter's criticism of Thomas More's *Utopia*:

> Even though here the devil hides his Gorgonian head under a thick veil of moral ideologies, this adds no charm to his countenance, and whoever lifts the veil will certainly be just as deeply shocked as at the sight of that hard picture of political realism, full of manly sincerity, which Machiavelli displays to us.[3]

In writing this book, I feel obliged to adhere closely to a similarly re

3

alistic attitude, with the proviso that some points of view will receive a stronger emphasis than has hitherto been the case, especially in the fields of geostrategy and psychological warfare.

In line with prevailing opinion, for many years I considered Hitler to be the main character in the drama of the Second World War, and held his policy of violent expansion and aggression to be the most important cause of its outbreak. Yet a more thorough analysis of the interplay of the main events has led me to the conviction that at the very least this viewpoint needed a radical modification. It became more and more apparent that Stalin was not only the real victor, but also the key figure in the war; he was, indeed, the only statesman who had at the time a clear, broadly-based idea of his objectives.

At this stage the objection will certainly be made that a study such as this is wrong-headed and should be rejected without further ado because it is attempting to exonerate Hitler. Readers will soon be able to judge for themselves that such a supposition is quite erroneous. The main question here at issue is rather to *reduce* the German dictator to his real political and intellectual stature and to correct the widely-accepted overestimation of his ability. This misapprehension had many causes: some of these are the spectacular impact made by his personal appearances, with long speeches in the theatrical atmosphere of mass rallies; his sabre-rattling rearmament of Germany and dramatic meetings with politicians; his acts of terror against people with other ideas than his, especially the Jews. But all this did not take place (as it did in the Soviet Union) in the far distance, behind a curtain rarely raised and even then only slightly, but right in the heart of Europe. People were kept on tenterhooks, terrified of surprises, trembling in their hopes for peace; and peace so obviously depended on the will of this one man . . . And then finally, by a single act of definite aggression, the dictator unleashed the war. After the victories of his breathtaking *Blitzkrieg* campaigns, and especially after the collapse of France, the strongest military power in Europe, the Führer was transformed into a fantastic figure, appearing to his frightened opponents as an almost superhuman phenomenon, who combined in one man the military genius of a Napoleon, the cunning of a Machiavelli and the fanaticism of a Mohammed. When the victors appeared as judges and prosecutors at the Nuremberg tribunal, Hitler was not personally on the bench with the accused; but he was considered to be the real originator of a unique crime in the history of humanity and thus once more, even though in a pejorative sense, he was elevated to extraordinary supereminence. To this must be added an additional element in the making of Hitler's reputation, and one which is often disregarded. Most German documents relating to the

4

war were published soon after the war ended; these were followed by a rapidly increasing number of memoirs and other writings seeking to explain what had happened; and it was also possible to interview surviving participants and victims: all this ensured that investigations into the war were fuelled by a complex array of facts and information. For the historian, the German dictator is a very tangible figure.

The reverse applies in the case of his opposite number in Moscow. Stalin was no friend of spectacular public appearances, but was certainly a master of the undercover game, of indirect action. Gafencu gives this characterisation:

> This man was cautious and calculating and prepared his blows with well-considered, patient cunning; he was also brutal and attacked with surprising quickness . . . He seemed to conspire with a world of mystery and for his seductive arts he preferred the glittering night of legend to the glaring light of publicity.[4]

There are other reasons why this character is not easily comprehensible. The sly, mistrustful Georgian probably did not confide even to his close associates what he knew, intended or desired. No less a person than General Schukov, Chief of the General Staff at the time, reports that Stalin probably withheld from him important military information just before the German invasion.[5] The red czar may, therefore, have taken many of his thoughts, secret and otherwise, into the grave with him; and even if the Russian archives are one day made accessible to free investigations, we still may not learn much from them.

For the time being, however, there can be no question of this happening, for such sources are only made available in accordance with the political interests of the time, and sensitive areas in particular can be the subject of massive disinformation, rendering well-authenticated judgement difficult. Because of this, conscientious research workers are unwilling to venture into an area where they are frequently dependent on surmises or clues – the term 'Kremlin astrology' is not completely without foundation.

Nevertheless, one cannot forgo the treatment of these important topics in the face of these difficulties, for that would mean capitulating to those who intentionally put them in our path. Moreover, the situation is in reality not quite as unfavourable as it seems. Even disinformation can offer important hints and clues, since it usually reveals which questions are especially sensitive, and the Soviets also have a favourite trick of blaming others for things they are doing themselves. Besides, the curtain has recently been raised a little in some places and in others it is a little more transparent than before.

It is worth remembering that even today the Second World War is often considered from the viewpoint of the anti-Hitler coalition, a position which has outlasted the rupture between the former allies and the ensuing Cold War. Moreover, Stalin's plans in the years 1939–41 were not only hindered but also covered up by the successes of the German army – which the Soviet dictator had failed to anticipate – in the first phase of the campaign in the East. Andreas Hillgruber has rightly pointed out that there are few grounds for agreeing with the Russian portrayal of their advance into Central Europe as a mere reaction to the German attack. Giving evidence going back to the autumn of 1940, he considers it to have been a large-scale programme 'to extend the Soviet sphere of influence in Europe – after making allowances for the defeat of Germany in the west – by taking up a frontal position against the USA and Great Britain extending into Central Europe'.[6] The proposition that Moscow had decided well in advance to take up an antagonistic posture against the Allied powers appears basically correct, but needs to be analysed in a more logical manner. The standpoint taken by Philipp W. Fabry is worth mentioning here, though it has as yet been given little credence: he suggests that the German dictator made himself dependent on the Soviet Union at the beginning of the war, and subsequently proved himself to be a useful tool in Stalin's campaign against the British and American 'capitalists'.

This standpoint accords with the fact, now seldom disputed in historical studies, that by granting Hitler cover on the eastern front by the agreement of 23 August 1939, Stalin made a decisive contribution to the confrontation between Germany and the Western powers which brought about the outbreak of the Second World War.

> It is ridiculous to try to maintain the assertion that, on ratifying the pact with Hitler, the Russian statesmen had not known that they were opening up for him a way into the war planned by them . . . a clever, Bolshevik policy, aiming at world revolution, must endeavour to make the Imperialists weaken each other, so that the Soviet Union increases its strength to be able to attack when the moment is ripe and give a forward thrust to the idea of world revolution.[7]

In this statement, revolutionary thought and the traditional Russian imperialism, dating from the czarist monarchy, work together in such a manner that it is almost impossible to separate these two components and balance the one against the other.

It must again be emphasised that this does not exonerate Hitler in any way, neither morally nor politically. On the contrary, his adventurous and unscrupulous actions, and they alone, enabled Stalin, from his position in the background, to steer a course towards war. The events of the summer of 1939 show the fateful consequences of Hitler's lack of statesmanlike qualities and a world-orientated political vision, and make him look very inferior to his Russian counterpart. With regard to political intelligence and political style, their relationship is like that of a gambler to a chess grandmaster, and the assertion that the Führer fell like a schoolboy into the trap set for him by Moscow can hardly be called exaggerated. The demonic Georgian had clearly needed to apply a hundred times more cunning in the internal struggles of the Soviet Communist Party than was required to bamboozle Hitler, not to mention the leaders of the Western powers.

If this gives the impression that Stalin was a key figure in the Second World War it does not imply that he was therefore its ultimate instigator. The fundamental causes of the catastrophe were not his work, nor could he have created them, though he showed stupendous skill in activating and exploiting them. But how he managed to manipulate the situations of the time to the political advantage of the Soviet Union has in many respects never been clarified satisfactorily. Even today much remains obstinately hidden beneath a veil of secrecy. Nonetheless, in spite of the often confusing and puzzling facade, an attempt will here be made to elucidate what amounts to a model lesson in sophisticated power politics, which by virtue of its inner unity and logical sequence is very impressive and in many respects still depressingly topical.

Mention has already been made of the Hitler–Stalin Pact. By now its motives have all been thoroughly explained, but at the time it evoked surprise, sensation and considerable confusion. National Socialism and Soviet communism had recently been bitterly fighting and blaspheming each other; yet now, suddenly, they appeared arm in arm. The agreement made a shattering impression on many with left-wing sympathies and also on many convinced Marxists and Communist Party members, since it appeared to be a betrayal of all ideological and political principles. In the West there were violent protests and even resignations from the Party; even in the Soviet Union plausible reasons had to be given for the Kremlin's decision. The fact of the matter was, however, that Stalin was seeking to bring about the outbreak of the 'imperialist war', in which the Soviet Union was initially to wait in her safely neutral position and achieve, with the least possible risk, the greatest possible advantage. An active incursion would only be contemplated later, when both parties were exhausted and no longer capable of offering effective resistance to the pressure of revolutionary progress – backed by the Red Army. Incidentally, Stalin had given utterance to similar thoughts in 1925:

> If war is to break out, we won't be able to watch in idleness; we will have to enter the fray, but we will be the last ones to do it, in order to put the decisive weight into the scales, a weight that should tip the balance.[8]

Yet this basic principle is in stark contrast with Molotov's behaviour during his Berlin visit in November 1940. As is well known, Stalin's ambassador not only made excessive demands, but also gave hints of future objectives which would, in practice, result in Germany being nothing more than a satellite of the Soviet Union. This revelation gave a decisive impetus to Hitler's plans for an attack on Russia. The behaviour of the foreign minister has variously been assessed as a serious mistake or a political puzzle:

> It is hard to define whether, in world-historical perspective, this revelation of Soviet future objectives was a blunder made by the usually taciturn Molotov, or whether it was a very sophisticated tactic, the point of which the historian finds hard to grasp.[9]

Closely connected with this is the thorny question as to whether Operation Barbarossa, Hitler's attack on the Soviet Union, was a preventive war. This theory is often objected to on the grounds that the idea was merely an invention of Nazi propaganda. But the German incursion into Norway was also justified, on the German side, by the assertion that a similar action by the enemy had to be anticipated, and at the time many people, including the author, believed this statement to be a propaganda manoeuvre; as things turned out, however, it was true. More pertinently, if Stalin wanted to remain neutral for as long as possible and only take an active part in the last phases of the war, then it is highly improbable that he intended to attack Germany at such an early stage of the conflict; it would have been more advantageous to wait long enough for the German army to be engaged on a second front in Europe. However, what we know of the development of the Red Army in the spring and early summer of 1941, though shrouded in secrecy on the Soviet side, speaks much more for than against the aggressive intentions of the Kremlin. The Soviet forces were certainly not completely on a war footing on the day Operation Barbarossa was launched, but evidence which must be taken seriously allows us to draw the conclusion that by late summer the preparations for a mass offensive against Germany would have been concluded and that such an attack was planned for 1942. The latter date was named by Stalin himself on 5 May 1941, in a private speech to officer cadets about which, unfortunately, we have only second-hand information (see page 100). It is very unlikely that Stalin expected this date to herald the last phase of the war.

Finally there is a further, possibly more difficult enigma. Through foreign sources and his own intelligence services, Stalin had excellent information about German plans and preparations for Barbarossa, but in spite of this he did nothing to guard his forces against the tactical surprise of the invasion. He even forbade precautionary measures on the grounds that they might provoke the Germans. When he did sound the alarm at the last moment, it came too late to be of any help to most of his forces. Was this incomprehensible behaviour due merely to a crude error made by a self-willed dictator, or did it conceal some 'secret Stalinistic manoeuvre'?[10]

At first sight all this seems confusing and contradictory enough. Nevertheless, as this book will now try to show, there is a red thread woven into the fabric of these events, a thread which represents a well-conceived policy, positioned with astonishing finesse and carried into practice in accordance with clear and logical principles. This proves Stalin to be a statesman of genius, far superior to his associates and opponents, and far superior to Hitler and those guiding the destiny of the Western powers. Admittedly, he too was not infallible, but his errors lay in the military, not in the political sphere: above all, he underestimated the striking power of the German army and overestimated the pace of his own rearmament. This led to the serious defeats of the summer and autumn of 1941 which finally thwarted the realisation of his ambitious plans – as will be discussed later (see page 64f.). Nonetheless, it was Stalin who emerged the real victor of the Second World War.

The evidence for that assertion will, I hope, emerge in the ensuing portrayal and analysis of the role played by the Russian dictator who, as a key figure in the Second World War, united the imperial heritage of the czars with the revolutionary principles of Marx and Lenin. In order not to overburden the work with already familiar material, the author will endeavour to treat only the most essential points of his argument in detail, leaving simply an outline of the remainder.

Imperialist Expansion

The traditionally pragmatic basis of Russian statesmanship has its roots far back in the Middle Ages, when Novgorod and later Moscow had to face up to threats from both east and west. This two-sided pressure led repeatedly to difficult political and military situations, which often brought great hardship in their wake. Alexander Nersky's victories over the Swedes and the German Order of Knights and Dmitri Donskoi's repulse of the two-pronged attack of the Tartar allies are both historical milestones. Besides the western opponents – Sweden and the United Polish–Lithuanian Empire – the threat in the south and south-west came from the Osmans pressing powerfully forward after the conquest of Constantinople. Since those days the Moscow rulers have always succeeded in playing their adversaries off against each other – by exploiting their conflicts of interest or by attacking their weaknesses through a skilful policy of alliances: as early as 1490 Ivan III formed an alliance with the emperor Maximilian I against Poland and Lithuania. By the Middle Ages, the Russians had become deeply suspicious of the Catholic west, at that time unified, which repeatedly attacked them in the rear as they struggled for survival in their wars against the Mongols.

Gradually, Russia achieved a higher status and became a force to be reckoned with in the European power game. During the Thirty Years War Gustavus Adolfus sought the support of Orthodox Russia against the Catholic powers: the Holy Roman Emperor, the Pope and Poland. The slow increase in the number of diplomatic and military successes led to a more dynamic expansionist policy – one no longer restricted to assembling Russian territories under the aegis of the czar, but beginning also to set its sights on more ambitious targets. In the struggle against Sweden and Poland–Lithuania the Russians made strenuous efforts to achieve dominance in the Baltic, while in the south and south-west the internal weakening of the Osman Empire offered them favourable chances for extending their influence, especially by playing on pan-Orthodox and pan-Slavonic sentiments. In 1655, for example, Czar

Alexei undertook the task of freeing all those of his faith from Turkish dominion, and at the same time the Croat priest Juraj Krizanic conceived the idea of a Slavonic Union, led by Moscow – although this idea was lumbered with a further plan to amalgamate Catholicism and Orthodoxy, which did not suit the Russians.[11] These happenings anticipated not only the rivalry with the Habsburg Empire, which since Prince Eugene's victories was also seeking to expand into the Balkans, but also the collision with Germany in the Baltic and south-east Europe.

These ambitious plans could only be realised in the course of the eighteenth century. Sweden was expelled from the Baltic and parts of Finland, Poland was divided and the Turks had to give up the northern coast of the Black Sea and recognise the czar's protective rights over the Danube Principalities, which later became Rumania. This made Russia the leading Baltic power, with an empire extending far to the west up to the Prussian and Austrian borders. The gateway to the Balkans had been pushed open, and beckoning them was their distant goal, the capital of the old Byzantine Empire, the 'Zargrad' of their traditions. But penetration into these regions infringed on English and French interests, giving rise to the 'Oriental question', one of the great problems of European politics and one which was to play an important role in the Napoleonic Wars.[12]

As time progressed, Austria became on the one hand an ally in the struggle against Turkey, but on the other hand an obstacle to the unrestricted extension of Russian influence in this region. At the outbreak of the war between Habsburg–Venice and the Turks in 1716, Peter the Great offered an alliance in Vienna, but a memorandum of the 'conference for Oriental affairs' told Karl VI to beware of the czar, who, 'using the pretext of an alliance, wouldn't hesitate to make unpleasant incursions into Moldau and Walachei', and 'whose influence in the neighbourhood, especially considering the great support he had in the Orient for religious reasons, must be watched with suspicion'.[13] Later, the clash of interests would become even more obvious. For example, State Councillor Rodofinikin, an agent for his country in Belgrade, forwarded in a memorandum of November 1808 an outline of future Russian policy in Serbia: the czar's empire must make sure that it had a predominant interest there in order to be able to attack Austria in the flank, if at any time Austria should become Russia's opponent.[14] In the further course of events, both Russia and the Serbs became imbued with the idea that both the Habsburg Empire and Turkey had to be destroyed if the Slavs were to gain their freedom.[15]

The victory over Napoleon opened up even more far-reaching prospects. Czar Alexander I not only considered himself to be the real con queror of the great Corsican and the saviour of Europe, but he also strove to achieve an indirect protectorate over the continent. His conception of the Holy Alliance consisted of a combination of pious and mystical philosophising – at first liberal but later very conservative – with a thoroughly down-to-earth power policy. This involved either putting Prussia and Austria under pressure by bringing Russia closer to post-Napoleonic France, or making them into junior partners of the eastern colossus within the framework of a pact of the conservative powers. Metternich, however, recognised these ulterior motives and missed no opportunity to thwart them. It was at this time that it also became apparent how far the aspirations of St Petersburg stretched into the Mediterranean area and to the west. When revolutions broke out in 1820 in Italy and Spain, probably abetted by undercover Russian agitation, the czar offered to send his troops to quell the uprisings, but for obvious reasons this suggestion was rejected. In the meantime, the two-faced nature of Russian policy was also evident in the case of Turkey. The Russian ruler asserted that he was the unequivocal champion of the legitimacy principle, which essentially favoured the Sultan. This firm principle was, however, somewhat compromised both by the support the Russians gave to the Greek uprising, and especially in the Treaty of Unkiar Skelessi (1833) which came about as a result of military pressure and took the form of a defensive alliance making Russia the only power protecting Turkey. Understandably this aroused the greatest mistrust in the other powers.

Great Britain particularly felt that its position in the east was threatened, and a wave of anti-Russian publicity developed there, laying foundations for a widespread and deep-rooted Russophobia. London now reacted with the greatest sensitivity to every action of St Petersburg which even remotely affected British interests, and promptly initiated counter-measures. The bitter quarrels between the greatest continental power and the mighty maritime empire had begun. These resulted in a clash of arms in the Crimean War of 1854–6, in which England and France blocked Russian aspirations to control over Turkey.

The confusion of countries opposing each other in the Balkans was further complicated by the entry of the German Empire and the Kingdom of Italy into the circle of interested powers, so that the region developed more and more into the powder keg of Europe. The attempt, through the war of 1877–8, to create a Greater Bulgaria dependent on Russia ended in failure, and at the Berlin Congress St Petersburg had to grant its rivals considerable concessions – without, however, giving up its long-term plans for the Balkans. These received a new impetus when, after the king's murder in June 1903 in Belgrade, the Russophile Karageorgevic dynasty came to power; and the tension between Serbia

12

and the Habsburg monarchy was further increased in the aftermath of the Austrian annexation of Bosnia and Herzegovina. Ultimately, of course, it was shots fired at Sarajevo that sparked off the First World War.

The reverses, often considered humiliating, which Russia had to accept in the second half of the last century sometimes resulted in a strengthening of patriotic, pan-Slavonic ideas – as reflected, for example, in Danilevski's famous book *Russia and Europe*.[16] Here, under the guise of science, a kind of all-embracing messianism was announced: the Germanic/Roman cultures were exhausted and would be succeeded by the Slavonic types which under Russian leadership would come to the forefront of world history. The fact remained, nevertheless, that the empire could extend no further to the west or south-west. In addition, the Russian incursion into central Asia in the last third of the century led to serious tension with Great Britain, and the British also encouraged Japan to oppose Russian expansion in the Far East. Meanwhile, a revolutionary situation had developed inside Russia as a result of unsatisfactory economic and social progress. The conservative politicians in St Petersburg believed they could avert this danger by a 'short and victorious war' against the Japanese; but instead of victory there were defeats on both land and sea, which hastened the outbreak of revolution in 1905.

In the end, the inflexible czarist system was no longer able to carry the burdens imposed upon it by the First World War. The unsolved social, economic and political problems, together with successive military reverses, offered a fertile soil to revolutionary propaganda, until eventually the Bolshevik revolution and the subsequent civil war made the powerful empire almost incapable of any action outside its borders. This led to the loss, once more, of large areas of the territories gained in the west: Finland and the Baltic States won their independence; a new Poland arose under French patronage – its eastern border pushed far forward into the White Russian and Ukrainian settlement areas; and Rumania annexed Bessarabia. It was the intention of the victors of the 1914–18 war that this belt of states should form a *cordon sanitaire* to protect Europe from Bolshevism and at the same time keep Germany in check from the east. However, a military incursion of the Western powers into this area would be fraught with difficulties, if only for geographical reasons. The entire arrangement was therefore only possible as a result of the weakening of Russia and Germany during the war, and could only be sustained as long as that lasted. If the Russians waxed powerful once more, it was to be expected that they would demand the return of these regions. So too, the borders decided on at Versailles, along with the German minorities they created, introduced a new and dangerous source of conflict into the geopolitical equation.

Furthermore, the decline of the Habsburg monarchy, which for so long had formed a barrier against Russian ambitions in the Balkans, had left a political vacuum which the great European states vied with each other to fill. France sought its support from the alliance between Yugoslavia, Rumania and Czechoslovakia directed against Hungarian wishes for a revised settlement, while the Italians wanted to bring the small states of Austria and Hungary into their sphere of influence. But it was only a question of time before Germany and the Soviet Union would be making their claims. With this in mind, Moscow sought to establish closer relations with Prague and so improve its position on the territory of the former monarchy. The Germans meanwhile, following the failure of the projected customs union with Austria in 1932 because of objections by the victorious powers, to some extent took over the mantle of the Habsburgs in the south-east – and with it their role as a bulwark against Russia – by the annexation of Austria in 1938. It can be seen that the Balkan problem also played its part in the breakdown of the Hitler–Stalin pact, though there are deeper underlying causes – particularly in the role Stalin envisaged for Germany in his plans for the future.

The newly-formed Soviet state initially had very great difficulties to contend with. In March 1918 it was forced to accept the Peace of Brest–Litowsk – of which one hard condition was the loss of the Ukraine, which was to serve as a granary for the central powers suffering from the blockade. Although these conditions lapsed at the end of the war, the confusion of the civil war and communist experiments put the already badly damaged economy into further disarray. To make matters worse, the hoped for revolution did not materialise and the Bolsheviks were forced instead to contend with the intervention of 'imperialist' forces. Whilst the Japanese sent in strong forces and pressed forward up to Lake Baikal, the actions of the other powers were fairly low-key. Nevertheless, the doctrine of the irreconcilable enmity between 'socialism' and 'capitalism' was one of the basic tenets of Bolshevism and the intervention gave it added weight and credibility. The 'Fatherland of all Workers' saw, or imagined, itself surrounded by a world of enemies seeking to destroy it by any available means.

These dangers were often greatly exaggerated for propaganda purposes and at times, if it seemed politically expedient, threats were even invented. For example, in secret session on 10 October 1917 the Central Committee decided, on Lenin's advice, to give a report on the situation which didn't correspond to the facts but furthered the political purposes of the revolutionary leaders. In this report a mutiny of German sailors was interpreted as 'the highest expression of the upsurge of the socialist world revolution throughout all Europe'. At the same time, 'the danger of a peace with the imperialists designed to strangle the

14

revolution in Russia' was declared, and the Kerenski government was accused of having made 'without any doubt, the decision to hand over Petrograd to the Germans'.[17] Whether Lenin believed these or similar assertions is very doubtful, but in any case it all lent momentum to the progress of the revolution. There was at the time no talk of intervention by the Allied powers, but Lenin knew very well how belief in an alleged 'world of enemies' could be used to mobilise and activate people.

Yet the intervention turned out to be anything but a resolute and well-organised attempt by the 'imperialists' to strangle the Russian revolution. All that took place was a series of half-hearted and ill coordinated actions, with virtually no large-scale engagements between the Red Army and Allied forces. The material support of the 'White' forces by the Western powers was certainly quite significant,[18] but on balance the intervention helped rather than hindered the Bolsheviks.

On the other hand, Lenin and his associates were never in any doubt about their determination to annihilate capitalism and 'imperialism'. They were convinced that the First World War was only the prelude to further 'imperialist wars', which would lead inexorably to the final victory of socialism across the whole world. What strategy the Soviet Union was to take during these altercations was clearly stated in Lenin's speech to the Action Meeting of the Moscow Organisation of the KPR (B) on 6 December 1920:

> Till the final victory of socialism in the whole world [the principle would apply] that we must exploit the contradictions and opposition between two imperialist power groups, between two capitalist groups of states and incite them to attack each other.[19] [If it should prove impossible to defeat both] then one must know how to group one's forces so that the two begin to fight each other, for when two thieves quarrel the honest man gets the last laugh. But as soon as we are strong enough to overthrow the entire capitalist world, we will seize it at once by the throat.[20]

Following on this Lenin sketched out three concrete examples of opposing interests which the Soviet policy could and should exploit. The first lay between Japan and America, the second between America and the remainder of the capitalist world, the third arose from the relationship between the Entente and a conquered Germany:

> This country cannot tolerate the treaty and must look round for allies to fight world imperialism, even though it is itself an imperialistic land, which is none the less being held down.[21] [It would in any case be most favourable] if the imperialist powers were to get involved in a war. If we are forced to tolerate such rogues as these capitalist thieves, each one of whom is sharpening the dagger against us, then it is our bounden duty to get them to turn their daggers on each other.[22]

15

The Soviet leader expressed similar thoughts shortly afterwards at the Eighth All-Russian Soviet Congress. These statements are of exceptional significance, for they represent not merely a piece of revolutionary rhetoric, but a statement of the principles of Soviet power policy which would remain authoritative for Stalin, and to a certain extent still apply today.

Lenin considered 'world imperialism' to be his main opponent, its main centres being obviously the strongholds of capitalism, England and America. In the beginning at least, England seems to have been considered the more dangerous:

> It was the proud bastion of world capitalism, the place from which radiated out, like concentric circles, all the threats of imperialism; it was the highest temple of international finance, the world centre of all the world's overseas trade, the metropole from where the peoples of the non-European world were sucked dry.[23]

The prospects of a revolution in the mother country were bad, and initially support for liberation movements in the British colonies seemed to offer the best chance of success. The clash of interests between English and Russian imperialism – an inheritance from the time of the czars – made this course of action doubly attractive.

The verdict on Germany is different, Lenin's expositions on the peace of Brest-Litowsk, which he had supported, are illuminating:

> It would appear that a kind of coalition has been formed between German imperialism and the first Socialist Republic against another kind of imperialism. But we have not made any coalition and have never taken any steps which might endanger or compromise the power of the Socialist State; we have so exploited the quarrel between the two imperialist groups that in the end both lost the game. Germany got nothing from the peace of Brest-Litowsk but a few million *pud* of grain, while in return Bolshevik disintegration was dragged into Germany. We, on the other hand, gained time to put the Red Army on its feet.[24]

This almost reads like an anticipation of Stalin's motives for his pact with Hitler, although when Lenin delivered that speech in December 1920 the National Socialists were an insignificant group. But tortured through war and want, Germany showed many signs of revolutionary unrest, and these were a great source of hope for Moscow. Prior to this, an incident took place which Lenin certainly found very disagreeable: when Radek, a member of the Bolshevik delegation, was arrested on 12 February 1919 in the Bolshevik propaganda office in Berlin, the police discovered an outline plan for a general communist offensive, which was to take place in the spring. According to the plan the Red Army was to march through Poland into Germany simultaneously with a German communist insurrection. A 'genuine revolutionary government' was to replace that of the Social Democrats Ebert and Scheidemann, ally itself with Russia on the Rhine and declare a new war against the 'imperialist allies'.[24a]

However, the Kremlin has never shunned working with German 'reactionaries' if there was ever any promise of an advantage. In any case, it was (and would remain) a principle of Russian power politics to keep Germany separated from the Western powers, to play them off against each other and embroil them in a war.

Just as Germany was set against England in Europe, similar tactics were used in the Far East in an endeavour to use Japan against the U.S.A. Lenin reported, not without some satisfaction, how he had already succeeded in this in the case of concessions in Kamchatka: 'To put it bluntly, we have incited Japan and America against each other and so gained an advantage'.[25] With the same intention, Stalin later guaranteed the Japanese a cover for their rear by the neutrality treaty of 13 April 1941, and so encouraged them to undertake military action against Great Britain and the U.S.A.

Thus Soviet foreign policy was, in the long term, dedicated to unleashing a new war between the imperialist powers – one which would weaken them and, more importantly, make them ripe for revolution. What in 1917 had only succeeded in Russia would later succeed in the metropolis of capitalism, and possibly throughout the whole world. This objective was also served by the so-called revolutionary defeatism, the assertion disseminated by agitators that the sole cause of war was the capitalist system, which had to be swept aside in order to clear a path for world peace under the banner of Soviet socialism. The real enemies were not the workers, the members of the same class opposing each other in the trenches, but the imperialist warmongers and war profiteers who ruled over them. The mutiny of war-weary soldiers combined with the insurrection of hungry masses of workers on both sides of the front would bring about the fraternisation of the proletariat on an international level and so a lasting peace. But the real purpose of all this was to exploit the longing for peace of people tormented by war – in order to effect, wherever possible, communist seizure of power under the patronage of Moscow.

However, these Marxist–Leninist thought processes should not be allowed to obscure the 'reasons of state': the legacy of the empire of the czars and the geostrategical position of Russia. Mention has already been made of the advances to the west and south-west; and to some extent one can also see the Holy Alliance as an attempt to integrate Prussia and Austria into the Russian sphere of influence. At the same time, however, these states – after 1871 the German Empire – represen

17

ted an obstacle to Russian ambitions, adopting policies of their own which did not accord with those of St Petersburg; they also blocked any thoughts of expansion as far as the Atlantic. But the mighty Russian Empire was also an Asiatic power, and would never be satisfied with being restricted to the north of the continent. As early as 1722–3 Peter the Great had led a war of conquest against Persia, and since then the pressure on that country had been maintained – with varied forces and variable success. An incursion into central Asia had taken place only in the last third of the previous century. But the big problem in the east was China, which at first was able to offer sustained resistance to Russian aggression. At the Treaty of Nortchinsk (1689) the Russians were even forced to give up, once again, the Amur region, gaining in return a stake in the lucrative trade with China. Only the internal collapse of the 'Empire of the Middle' enabled foreign powers to gain greater influence in the territory of the weakened state, resulting in rivalry between England and France, joined later by Japan and the U.S.A. At the turn of the last century Russia succeeded in considerably augmenting her power base in the Far East, especially by the military occupation of Manchuria during the Boxer Rebellion and the leasing of the Liaotung Peninsula, including the ice-free harbour of Port Arthur. Although the Russo–Japanese war, which resulted in the loss of Port Arthur and the southern portion of Sakhalin Island, was a severe reverse, the czarist empire contrived, shortly before the outbreak of the First World War, to make Outer Mongolia into a kind of protectorate, whilst recognising the sovereignty of China. During this period the centre of gravity of Russian policy lay in the west, where the German Empire occupied a special position because of its military and industrial might. As the strongest continental power, it was both a dangerous potential opponent, and also a valuable ally – if it could be made dependent on Russia. As such it formed the key to the mastery of the continent of Europe.

Max Weber, not only the greatest German sociologist but also a gifted political thinker, warned of the consequences of such dependency as long ago as the time of the First World War. In his essay 'Bismarck's foreign policy and the present', written in 1915, he expressed strong views on the subject, warning especially against making an enemy of Britain:

> Whilst England can threaten our trade and overseas possessions and France the territory we own, Russia is the only power which, in the case

of a victory, would be in a position to threaten not only our political independence, but also the very fabric of the Polish as well as the German nationality. This will apply to an even greater extent in the future.[26]

It would be dangerous for Germany to adopt a policy of annexation, which could only lead to one result: 'Germany's boots in Europe would be standing on everyone's toes'.[27] In all this it was most important to be able to assure the western Slavonic people that in avoiding rape by Russia they would not have to suffer rape by Germany instead.[28] In his study a year later entitled *Germany amongst the European World Powers*, Weber stated:

> It is certainly not desirable that we should make Russia our permanent enemy in the future. Nor is it desirable that instead of having France alone as an enemy, we have France and England. For in this case, Russia could impose on us its own conditions for any agreement. It would have us in its pocket, we would be its tool.

This danger was also clearly recognised by Metternich. He too

> opposed in the spring of 1824 the attempt by Russia to induce Austria to break its entente with England and to form a closer relationship with the 'trois souverains de l'alliance'. He did not intend to break off the English connection and thus deliver himself up to Russia with his hands tied.[29]

Max Weber warned of the very things which the Soviets later planned and which the shortsightedness and dilettantism of Hitler and Ribbentrop allowed them to achieve: to make Germany dependent on the Soviet Union so that she could be used as a weapon against the Western allies, who were stronger and more dangerous in the long run; and finally, when she had served her purpose, to be liquidated as an independent power.

Admittedly, the victors of 1918 assisted considerably in the progress of this strategy. The Treaty of Versailles tore open a gulf between Germany and the West which made the Polish policy envisaged by Weber more difficult to carry out, and also engendered a revengeful attitude, which in the end really did bring about a position where the German jackboot was standing on everyone's toes. Instead of showing friendship to the young German democracy and carefully encouraging it, the Allies, especially France, did great damage to it by intrigue and excessive reparation demands, and played into the hands of a propaganda which defamed the democratic politicians as 'November criminals' and traitors. Where political vision and a sense of statesmanlike responsibility were needed, the victors showed only feelings of bitterness and vengeance instead. Consequently, men like Walter Rathenau, who wanted least of all a separation from the West by a union with Russia, found themselves finally forced to seek some backing from the Russians at Rapallo in 1922. George F. Kennan has since criticised, with the sharpness it deserves, the attitude of the Allies at that time. He condemned the thoughtlessness displayed by the Western democracies in dealing with the moderate and sincere elements of the Weimar Republic and further criticised the completely inappropriate manner in which they frittered away the co-operation of these elements with the interests of the West. And he noted the iron logic of the circumstances where an emotional and vengeful anti-German feeling in the Western nations played into the hands of the Soviet politicians.[30]

In itself, the treaty signed at Rapallo did not contain anything sensational: it merely arranged for the resumption of full diplomatic relations between the two powers, the mutual annulment of compensation claims and the conceding of 'most-favoured-nation' clauses. There were neither military agreements nor secret additional clauses. Nevertheless, the agreement was a considerable success for Soviet diplomacy in that it succeeded, if on a modest scale, in playing Germany off against the Western powers and so putting pressure on them.

But Berlin was far from dependent on Moscow. This was soon demonstrated when the foreign-policy-makers of the Weimar Republic, especially Gustav Stresemann, sought to reach an understanding with the victorious powers and achieved most of what they asked for – after long-drawn-out and tedious negotiations. Although Stresemann was not thinking of a break with the Soviet Union and even concluded a treaty of friendship with the Soviets in 1926, his doings were looked upon there with mistrust and suspicion, for they did not fit in with the intention of using Germany to oppose the Western democracies.

The Soviets also sought to benefit from the discrimination against Germany in the Versailles Treaty by offering the German army facilities for manoeuvres and exercises on their territory. In this way the Germans could evade some of the restrictions imposed upon them, while the Russians could benefit from German military technology and theory. This co-operation, which began in 1921, lasted up to Hitler's rise to power, in spite of difficulties and crises.[31]

The subversive activities of the Communist International were, however, a very palpable aggravation of German–Soviet relations. This organisation had already supported various uprisings in Germany during the early post-war years and was still continuing its operations, even after the hopes of an early revolution had vanished and both nations had won diplomatic recognition. Complaints about these subversive activities were returned by the Soviet foreign commissariat with the re mark that the Soviet state was not responsible for the actions of the Comintern.[32] A similar double strategy was adopted in other states which had taken up diplomatic relations with Moscow.

Taken as a whole, then, the Soviet Union's German policy was not initially a great success. As a result the Kremlin did try to improve its relations with the Western powers, but the atmosphere of mistrust was not easily swept away and its achievements were modest. The attempt to incite one state against another had failed, for the time being, and Soviet policy gravitated back towards internal affairs – especially the accelerated industrialisation programme and the enforced collectivisation of agriculture.

The 'Second Imperialist War'

All this changed at the beginning of the thirties. Slowly a situation was developing which would finally enable Stalin to make use of Hitler to cause the outbreak of the 'Second Imperialist War'. This situation was not set in motion in Europe, however, but in east Asia. Although the Japanese had withdrawn troops stationed on Soviet territory as part of the Allied intervention, they sought to maintain and extend their influence on the continent, assisted by the temporary weakness of the Soviet Union and the permanent weakness of China. For their part, the Soviet revolutionary leaders had at first condemned the czarist expansionist policy towards the Empire of the Middle as 'imperialist', and announced that the unjust treaties which St Petersburg had made with Peking were null and void: in future all dealings with China were to be carried out on a basis of equality. These generous declarations were probably made with the ulterior motive of restraining the Chinese from supporting the White Guards Army of Admiral Koltschak in Siberia. Certainly Moscow forgot its noble intentions soon after the defeat of Koltschak. Once more it set about extending its influence in China, if only to oppose that of the English and especially the Japanese.

With this in mind, the Soviet leaders sought to make use of Chinese nationalist and 'anti-imperialist' forces, with the intention of destroying them when the time was ripe. Accordingly, the communists allied themselves with the revolutionary nationalist Kuomintang Movement, founded by Sun Yat-sen, one of the most outstanding figures in the history of modern China. When he died in 1925 he was succeeded by General Chiang Kai-shek. This officer, who was trained in Moscow, saw through the Kremlin's ploys and so built up a powerful army with their help. This force proved its worth at the Shanghai revolt in 1927: the city was in the hands of opponents of the Kuomintang, but when the general moved up his forces there was a communist revolt. At first he halted his forces in front of the city and waited till the communists had won. Then, at their invitation, he moved into the city and ruthlessly massacred his communist 'allies'. This was a grim reverse for Soviet foreign policy in China, which was already by then the responsibility of Stalin.

Moscow suffered an equally serious setback when the Japanese, exploiting a favourable situation in Manchuria, moved their troops in and established the puppet state of Manchuko in March 1932; the Soviets were even forced to sell the East China Railway – which they had built at the time of the czars and had since kept possession of – to the fledgling state. Later various incidents took place, especially on the borders of Manchuko and Outer Mongolia (now again ruled by Moscow). Hostilities increased and in the summer of 1939 finally led to the Battle of the River Chalchin Gol, where strong forces were put in by both sides. The Soviets gained a victory which demonstrated the efficiency of the Red Army and convinced the Japanese that they had an opponent which must be taken seriously. At the same time the Japanese expansionist policy – which was partly driven by overpopulation on the islands – took on global importance as it began to damage various English and American interests. A League of Nations investigative committee, chaired by the Englishman Victor Lytton, was set up to examine the situation. When the Lytton Report was accepted in February 1933 by the full assembly in Geneva, the Japanese delegation marched from the hall, watched in embarrassed silence by the remaining members.

At this time Hitler was already Chancellor of the German Empire. More than enough has already been written about this man, his origins, his meteoric ascent to power and his final downfall, so here a few short remarks may suffice. In one respect Hitler was an arrant failure: he had no training for any employment; he either couldn't or didn't want to establish himself in any trade or profession; and after four years' service in the army he hadn't even managed to reach the rank of NCO. A person with Bohemian tendencies and artistic inclinations – but lacking any noticeable talent – he was a stranger to regular, disciplined work, and could never manage to do any even when in the responsible position of Chancellor of the Empire. In the presence of the 'higher classes', the aristocracy and the officer corps, the Führer was full of uncertainty – perhaps, indeed, in his heart he desired their downfall – so that attempts by nationalist, conservative and 'capitalist' circles to engage him for their purposes ended in complete fiasco. Faced by the notorious dwindling of party funds during the war Hitler certainly took donations from these sources, but he never thought of accepting any 'advice'.[33] After he had risen to the position of dictator, these groups were not expropriated and physically liquidated, as in Russia, but were for the most part rendered impotent.

Undoubtedly the man from Braunau was not a bad tactician. General Halder later attributed to him an almost animal-like instinct in scenting out power relationships,[34] not only in dealing with opponents, but also with members of his own party, whom he could skilfully outmanoeuvre and if need be brutally eliminate. Above all, however – unlike bourgeois politicians – he was a master of the art of mass demagogy and even boasted of having learnt his techniques from the Bolsheviks.[35] His success in finally seizing power was achieved by exploiting to the full the economic crisis, the fear of communism and the general disintegration of political life. The totalitarian trap had closed its jaws. The dominant power of the National Socialists could no longer be dissolved by democratic means, but the German Army only noticed the danger when it was too late. No general verdict can be given on this: many people, especially the young, joined the movement under the pressure of need, but also full of sincere idealism. They expected it to bring their salvation – and real successes really were achieved, especially in reviving the economy and ending most of the unemployment. The price that had to be paid for this was only found out later.

Hitler had undeniable capabilities and sometimes came up with ideas good enough to even astonish experts, but for a statesman he was notably lacking in perceptive powers and a sense of responsibility, so that in the end he groped his way into the trap set for him by Stalin and into a war which, from a military and a political point of view, was beyond his abilities and which led to his downfall. To understand the problematical nature of this man, who was a creature of crisis, one must delve into the innermost part of his personality: the 'toughest German of all time' was a fundamentally unstable character with distinct psychopathic traits, who at times broke down in critical situations. Hidden behind the mask of the dictator–redeemer were uncertainty, sentimentality, even lacrimosity – in the end he didn't seek death on the field of battle, like General von Fritsch, but crept away from history in his bunker–grave.

Whether Hitler simply wanted war cannot be answered unambiguously, though most people suppose otherwise. Certainly he often talked of war, decided on a military style of education for young people, ordered rearmament and often enough announced his intention to expand the armed forces. He also used threats of war to carry on a most dangerous game of chance, in which at first he was helped again and again by the retreat of his opponents. But his behaviour at the handing over of the British ultimatum (see page 39) gives some idea that in his heart he had a deep fear of matters becoming serious.

Although the Führer's views on foreign affairs changed to some ex-

24

tent in the course of time, there was hardly any divergence on the all-important points. Originally France was held to be the main enemy, and attempts were made to improve relations with the British, who were not in favour of French hegemony on the continent. But Hitler's ideas on the subject were vague and contradictory. The prerequisite for reaching an agreement with Britain was that Germany should share in a European balance of power or collective security system, and so renounce any claims to predominance. This was untenable for Hitler since it ran counter to the far-reaching expansionist policy in the east by which he intended to create a vast *Lebensraum* for the German people. Hitler was deluding himself when he thought he could obtain at least the tacit consent of England for these plans, for clearly they could not be implemented without German hegemony on the continent. In any case these aspirations, which had been partly anticipated by the German eastern policy of 1917–18, could only have been satisfied at the expense of Poland and especially of the Soviet Union, which was considered to be an enemy not only for ideological but more importantly for ethnic reasons. Following on the discrimination and pogroms in czarist Russia, or attracted by the messianic announcements of Karl Marx, there were numerous Jews amongst the theorists, leaders and supporters of the Russian Revolution, for which reason Hitler considered Moscow to be the centre of a 'Jewish-Bolshevik world conspiracy'. Added to this was the idea of the so-called racial inferiority of the Slavs, who were therefore expected to be the slaves of a German master race. This dogma contributed to a serious underestimation of the Red Army as well as to the senseless and brutal policy of occupation in the conquered eastern territories.

Some time ago, at the suggestion of Gauleiter Koch, Hitler had been pondering the idea of an alliance with Russia against Poland. He did not, however, see such an alliance as a lasting solution to the problem of mastery over Europe, for Germany and Russia could never become one great entity, ruling the world:

> Then we would really mistrust each other, and such a pact would inevitably end in a decisive battle. Only one of us can rule, and if we are to be the one we must defeat Russia. It must not be forgotten that Russia is not only the land of Bolshevism, but also the greatest continental empire of the world, with an impetus powerful enough to pull all Europe with it. The Russians take over their partner, body and soul, that is the danger; one can either give oneself over to them completely, or steer well clear of them.[36]

When things reached a critical juncture Hitler brought ruin on himself by not steering well clear; instead he made himself dependent on Moscow, with dire consequences.

In his foreign policy the dictator first moved cautiously to stabilise his rule inside Germany and to gain time for rearmament. Repeatedly he stressed his desire for peace with all nations, including Russia. He said, for example, in a speech on 23 March 1933, that the German government was willing to have friendly relations with the Soviet Union and that this would be beneficial to both.

> The struggle with communism in Germany is our internal affair, and we will never submit to foreign interference in this. Our political relationship to other powers with whom we have common interests will not be affected by this.[37]

Hitler's first priority was to gain respectability in the field of foreign affairs by means of international agreements and to conceal his ulterior motives. The first of these was the concordat with the Vatican in July 1933, which was followed by the non-aggression pact with Poland in January 1934 and the naval agreement with England in June 1935.

However, signs of the conflicts to come soon appeared. To begin with many people had thought that the Hitler regime would soon collapse, but National Socialist Germany emerged with increasing self-confidence and grew instead into a power to be reckoned with. The Germans followed the Japanese in leaving the League of Nations, and when that body imposed economic sanctions against Italy for the invasion of Abyssinia, its relations with Rome were seriously affected. These sanctions, half-heartedly agreed upon at England's suggestion and even more half-heartedly implemented, didn't prevent Mussolini's conquest of Abyssinia, but did lead to a closer rapprochement between Hitler's Germany and Italy. One blow then followed another. In March 1936 German troops, flagrantly breaking the Treaty of Versailles, marched into the demilitarised Rhineland. Only a few battalions were involved and a French counter-action could easily have driven them out, but the gambler in the imperial chancellery had bet on the weakness and confusion of his opponents and won – not a shot was fired. The Western powers suffered a serious loss of prestige and in the administrations of many European states the opinion was spread round that, for better or for worse, some agreement would have to be made to cope with the increasing power of the dictators.

Soon after this, civil war broke out in Spain, which was already suffering from economic ills and social tensions. The conflict soon became a kind of dress rehearsal for the Second World War. Hitler and Mussolini intervened in support of the rebellious General Franco, and in

26

October 1936 they formally united their two countries in the Berlin–Rome Axis. A month later this alliance was extended by the Japanese entry into the Anti-Comintern Pact. This agreement was directed not only against subversive activities and the Soviet Union, but also against the Western democracies, who supported the Spanish Republicans, though without much enthusiasm. The English Conservative government was particularly reticent, while the French Popular Front government had its sphere of action severely restricted. The Soviets, on the other hand, were more deeply engaged, with strong forces engaged in the fighting. But broadly speaking, the animosity of the Anti-Comintern Pact members towards the democratic powers was not due to events in Spain or for ideological reasons: it was rather because they were, or considered themselves, disadvantaged and demanded a share in the wealth and territories which their rivals possessed. Consequently, though Moscow felt threatened by the Anti-Comintern Pact, it did not neglect the possibilities inherent in the tension between the two alignments of capitalist states: the haves, gorged with possessions, and the have-nots, with their aggressive demands. There were now very promising reasons for 'inciting against each other' these two groups of 'imperialist' powers, exactly as Lenin had intended, and for using one as a stick with which to beat the other.

It remained a basic principle of Soviet foreign policy to work actively against any approaches made by Germany to the Western democracies. For this reason the Kremlin was hostile towards the liberal Weimar Republic, and the moderate German Social Democrats were the target of especially virulent attacks. It is ironic that these attacks helped the National Socialist cause, at least indirectly. It is possible that Moscow hoped that fascism, the most extreme form of capitalism, would lead by a dialectical reversal into communism; but it is also possible that they encouraged the inner disruption of Germany as a prelude to taking over power themselves. Furthermore, the peace-loving Weimar Republic was considered to be a completely unsuitable instrument for unleashing the 'Second Imperialist War'. In this respect, Hitler was a far more promising prospect.

For a time Stalin's attitude towards Hitler's Germany was remarkably reticent, even though the National Socialist terror was directed with especial rigour against the communists. Only slowly did he become aware of the danger which might threaten from this quarter. The German–Polish non-aggression pact in particular must have had an unsettling effect in Moscow, and it became the object of Soviet foreign policy to isolate the Führer, whose ideas of expansion towards the east were well known. It was decided to approach the Western powers, and also all political forces which rejected fascism or felt threatened by it. In Sep-

27

tember 1935 the Soviet Union joined the League of Nations and in May 1935 mutual assistance pacts were concluded with France and Czechoslovakia. At the same time the Comintern made a complete change of course: a people's front was to be formed under the banner of anti-fascism. As broadly based as possible, it would welcome not only democratic socialists, hitherto bitterly attacked, but also all kinds of bourgeois sympathisers. In this way the Kremlin hoped to increase its influence throughout Europe, and prevent a rapprochement between Germany and the Western democracies.

The success of this policy cannot be denied, especially in France where the moderate left, after some hesitation, agreed to co-operate. In the spring of 1936, a Popular Front government was elected, led by Léon Blum, socialist and humanist, and pupil and admirer of Jean Jaurès, who had been murdered in 1914 because of his opposition to the First World War. With this background, Blum could only advocate increased rearmament after slowly struggling free of his pacifist ideals. In Spain, on the other hand, the electoral victory of the People's Front led to a right-wing revolt and civil war. Whereas the governments of the democratic nations, especially Britain, tended to exercise restraint, anti-fascist propaganda in the 'pink thirties' was favourably received by young Western intellectuals, and by public opinion generally in the Anglo-Saxon nations. In many countries young people with various shades of left-wing opinions – by no means only communists – decided to join the International Brigade and risk their lives in the struggle against Franco, or at least to work as reporters for the cause of the People's Front. It would not be much of an exaggeration to say that Republican Spain became the focal point of the intellectual elite of the West – provided they were to the left of centre – attracting names as diverse as George Orwell and Ernest Hemingway. On the other hand, the Spanish Civil War brought Hitler and Mussolini closer together, rendering the polarisation between fascism and democracy complete.

Things were, however, not quite so simple, and in considering the alignment of powers during the war in Spain it is, initially at least, impossible to anticipate the anti-Hitler coalition of 1941 with any certainty. The People's Front was regarded in influential circles as an extension of Moscow's powers, compared with which fascism was the lesser evil; and in fact acts of terror were much worse in Russia than in Mussolini's Italy, while the most frightful excesses of Hitler's Germany were still a thing of the future.[38] Indeed, the British government was giving clandestine support to Franco, though perhaps with the secret motive of preventing him from becoming completely beholden to Hitler and Mussolini.[39] Reverses occurred, however, even in the ideological field. The brutality and unscrupulousness displayed by exponents of

Soviet communism in taking over key positions in Republican Spain and suppressing all other left-wing groups, together with the big show trials in the Soviet Union, had a very sobering effect on many communists and fellow travellers in the West. Up to that time, these people had still believed in the emancipatory character of Marxism and the humanistic core of the Russian Revolution; Now they had serious doubts. Eventually the Hitler–Stalin Pact would, in the majority of cases, bring about the final rupture with the 'god who failed'.[40]

The wave of purges by which Stalin instilled fear into the whole of Russia at that time can be called without exaggeration the most massive communist persecution of all times, for it demanded more victims, and above all more prominent victims, than all the terror of the counter-revolution. A horrifying number of the old guard of Bolshevism, leading party and state functionaries, the intelligence services, the secret police and even Comintern members were condemned to death, or they simply disappeared for ever, on the most spurious grounds. No one was safe in the course of this witches' sabbath, and the judge and hangman of one day were accused and liquidated the next. The armed forces, especially the generals and commanders, were badly hit. Such a blood-bath took place that the Red Army may have suffered a greater loss of officers through these purges than through the entire course of the Second World War. It will never be possible to define precisely the motives which induced Stalin to order such a slaughter. It is, however, most probable that the dictator, having in mind the future strife amongst world powers, decided to put aside every possible rival, to nip in the bud every conceivable opposition, to ensure for himself in all quarters slavish obedience and then to fill any vacant positions with his own puppets. These happenings doubtless for some time lowered the prestige of the Soviet Union, severely prejudiced the reputation of the Soviet armed forces in the eyes of the other powers, thus reducing the nation's usefulness as an ally and therefore perceptibly weakening the political status of Moscow. It can be assumed, however, that Stalin was prepared to pay the price of such repercussions in order once and for all to be in complete command of the internal political situation. It is remarkable that although the lowered reputation of the Red Army damaged Soviet interests, in certain respects it also helped them – and quite considerably: those acting for and against Stalin – Hitler as well as the leaders of the Western powers – did not fully appreciate the danger which threatened them from this quarter. Whether this was all part of Stalin's calculations will never be answered.

Although the Soviets had given considerable support to Spain, this help was later greatly reduced. It is possible that Stalin wanted to avoid any foreign policy complications during the purges, and therefore felt disinclined to make the British even more mistrustful by supporting any large-scale operations. A further possibility is that he wanted to draw out the conflict in order to tie down German and Italian forces and keep the fires of discontent burning. At the same time the Soviet dictator may have been thinking, while civil war still raged in Spain, of reaching an agreement with Hitler's Germany.[41]

The Western powers have often been bitterly reproached for not standing up to Hitler at the right time, which would have been possible with little risk at the time of the Rhineland occupation. With hindsight, these reproaches are certainly justified. Yet neither in England nor France did either people or government want a preventive war, and in the U.S.A. at the time isolationism ruled the field unopposed. The heavy sacrifices of the First World War were far from forgotten, and pacifist ideas exercised great influence, especially among left-wingers – this was the era of the Oxford Union debating society's resolution declaring that members were not willing to fight for king or country.[42] This attitude was not limited to students and intellectuals, but was shared by many circles and groups. Liberals and Labour Party members were particularly vociferous in urging Britain to reduce her armaments for the sake of peace, and even remained unperturbed by a setback as serious as Germany's withdrawal from the League of Nations. These tendencies became even more pronounced in the autumn of 1933 when Labour, using pacifist slogans, won a triumphant by-election victory in which the Conservatives suffered heavy losses. Now the Labour Party begin in earnest to demand complete disarmament, and through fear of losing more votes the Tories had to do the same.[43] Winston Churchill, who saw the storm brewing, found himself virtually isolated in his own party. About this depressing situation he wrote later:

> Delight in smooth-sounding platitudes, refusal to face unpleasant facts, desire for popularity and electoral successes irrespective of the vital interests of the State, genuine love of peace and pathetic belief that love can be its sole foundation, obvious lack of intellectual vigour in both leaders of the British Coalition Government . . . the strong and violent pacifism which at this time dominated the Labour–Socialist Party, the utter devotion of the Liberals to sentiment apart from reality . . . all these constituted a picture of British fatuity and fecklessness which, though devoid of guile, was not devoid of guilt and, though free from wickedness or evil design, played a definite part in the unleashing upon the world of horrors and miseries which, even so far as they have unfolded, are already beyond comparison in human experience.[44]

Admittedly, the appeasement policy, later severely criticised, was based not only on pacifist illusions but also on more practical considerations of a political and military nature. For a long time Britain's involvement with the Commonwealth hindered any significant engagement on the continent. It was known in London that an altercation, at one and the same time, with Germany, Italy and Japan would place Britain in a most difficult situation, and there was no certainty as to the reactions of individual dominions in the case of a new European war. There was some hope of backing from America, but this helper might later take on the role of heir. There were also sound economic arguments for a policy of restraint. Large sections of British industry suffered from structural weaknesses and were in need of modernisation, the country's competitiveness on the world market had worsened, and the balance of payments was showing a growing deficit. How could one expect an economy just recovering from a great depression to take on the burden of rearmament?[45] There was also some fear in Conservative circles that a war would result in a social revolution, so an understanding with Hitler's Germany was recommended, National Socialism being judged a lesser evil than Bolshevism. However, fascism could never have taken root in England. Oswald Mosley, his party and supporters never occupied anything more than a peripheral position. The real message of all this was an expression of helplessness in the face of the totalitarian threat: The description, 'a policy of impotence', is not inappropriate.[46]

Even more significant was the decline in the power of France. That country had suffered greatly in the First World War, and also lost a large part of its foreign investments. After a recovery in the twenties the world economic crisis was being felt there too, and as the country was behind the times both industrially and socially internal political tensions were increasing. Unlike England there were significant forces on the right giving more or less open support to fascism; but there was also a strong Communist Party. This made the land a prey to the psychological warfare of Hitler and Stalin. In the military sphere the main emphasis was on defence. When de Gaulle, a lieutenant-colonel at the time, recommended setting up an army of motorised shock troops with tanks, his suggestion fell on deaf ears. Instead, France had entrenched itself behind the Maginot Line, which was constructed at a staggering cost and eventually proved completely useless. This passive attitude did not remain unnoticed and one European state after another sought to come to the best possible arrangements with the aggressive dictators. In 1936 even Belgium withdrew from its alliance with its southern neighbour and assumed neutral status. France lost all support on her borders as the country weakened and could offer no real help.[47]

The most disastrous result of this development was, however, that the dictators became more and more convinced that England and France had no longer the will nor the ability to oppose with arms their plans for conquest.

Prelude to Catastrophe

Events in the year 1937 seemed to proceed fairly calmly. Stalin was fully occupied with his purges and at the beginning of the year Hitler had declared that the time for surprises was over. Nonetheless, the bloodshed in Spain was continuing, and in the Far East tension between China and Japan had turned into open warfare, the Japanese army making advances deep into China.

However, the dramatic events of the following year were already casting shadows before them. On 5 October 1937 Hitler informed his senior military and political advisers that he had decided to use force to solve the problem of Germany's need for territorial expansion – the German 'space problem' as he called it. This didn't mean simply drawing up a plan of war – an outline of co-ordinated political, military and economic preparations – but rather making a general declaration of intent, aimed directly at Austria and especially Czechoslovakia. Hitler based his proposals on the assumption that the Western powers would stand idly by if he resorted to force against these two countries. This view was not shared by Generals von Blomberg and von Frisch, who doubted the possibility of localising an armed conflict in Europe and warned that it would develop into a large-scale war which would be far beyond Germany's capabilities[48]. The upshot was that Hitler got rid of Blomberg and Frisch – the latter by means of a most unsavoury intrigue – and on 4 February 1938 took over personally as supreme commander of the armed forces.

It was now becoming more and more obvious that Hitler's objectives went beyond a revision of the dictates of the Treaty of Versailles: he also intended to establish German hegemony on the continent of Europe. But in doing so he was overestimating the British aversion to military involvement in Europe: he thought that London was prepared, for better or for worse, to give him a free hand; he was not seeking to destroy the Commonwealth, which would in any case ultimately benefit other powers, especially America and Japan. France, robbed of all influence in Europe, was to be restricted to its own territory and so relegated to the status of a second-rate power. Lastly, Fascist Italy was intended for the role of junior partner, with increasing dependence on Germany. The Führer believed, however, that London and Paris would not see through his plans, or that if they did they would not offer any serious resistance to them. He was even right at first: Britain and France didn't lift a finger when he advanced into Austria.

As a result of the forcible annexation of that country, Czechoslovakia found itself in a very unfavourable strategical position which Hitler at once set about exploiting ruthlessly. He was admittedly now confronted by a much more difficult problem than hitherto, for the Czechoslovakia of Masaryk and Benes was well-armed, protected by strong fortifications and had treaties of alliance with France and the Soviet Union. Because of this the danger of an armed clash in Europe became increasingly real and was a cause of serious worry to the German general staff. Its chief, Ludwig Beck, resigned and warned of the possibility of a new war:

> A war begun by Germany will at once involve other countries as well as the one attacked. In a war against a world coalition Germany would lose and then be subjected to the whims and caprices of the victors.[49]

Although Beck's strategic analysis proved right in the end, the gambler was once again successful in the early stages. After dramatic negotiations the Western powers again drew back, sacrificed Czechoslovakia, and so frustrated the plan of German opposition groups to use the dreaded catastrophe to topple the dictator. The Soviet Union alone expressed willingness to help Czechoslovakia, but this had no practical significance as the two countries had no common border and Poland and Rumania refused to allow their territory to be used in any way by Russian troops. Indeed, the Russian offer to help only served as an additional argument for those who suspected that Czechoslovakia was the end of Moscow's long arm reaching into Europe. That is why Chamberlain, who deeply distrusted the Russians, was not at all sorry that the Munich Agreement was fixed without their participation.

This agreement cannot, however, be regarded as a complete capitulation on the part of the Western powers. Politicians, especially in London, were hoping that Hitler would be satisfied with his substantial and bloodless successes and agree to participate in a new system of collective security. Such considerations were by no means completely without foundation. An overwhelming majority of the public in Germany – as also in Britain and France – were afraid of war; indeed, many prominent Nazis were also opposed to new adventures, not just because of moral scruples but also because they did not wish to jeopardise the comfortable prosperity given them by the National Socialist revolution.

Furthermore, even Mussolini had been exercising a moderating influence on his German colleague in an effort to prevent a crisis.

But Hitler and many of his henchmen had no intention at this stage of holding back and taking the last chance of a peaceful settlement. They even felt strengthened in their contempt for the Western statesmen, those ridiculous 'umbrella politicians'. *Hubris* and *Ate*, overweening pride and dazzling delusion, had set their ominous machinery in motion.

The gambler, having hitherto enjoyed a most improbable and extraordinary run of luck, continued his high-risk game – but now the stakes were higher. In so doing he removed the last shreds of credibility from the policy of 'appeasement', by which he had profited enormously. The ink of the signatures on the Munich Agreement was hardly dry when the dictator delivered an aggressive speech in Saarbrücken, for no obvious reason; and when shortly afterwards the German ambassador in Paris was murdered by a Jewish assailant this was used as a reason, or rather an excuse, for unleashing a new wave of Jewish persecution, which was far worse than any previously experienced. In the *Reichskristallnacht* of 9–10 November 1938 shop fronts were smashed in so-called spontaneous anti-Jewish riots which were in reality centrally organised. In addition, new legal restrictions were announced which made it well-nigh impossible for Jews to earn a living. Thus any hopes of conciliatory moves were immediately smashed in a most spectacular fashion.

Any lingering doubts about Hitler's intentions were finally removed by the march on Prague in March 1939. If there might have been some slight justification for the Munich Agreement on ethnic grounds or for strategic purposes in defence of Germany's flank, no such arguments could apply to this act of aggression and extortion. As late as 1938 Hitler had declared that he didn't want any Czechs and that the truncated state did not constitute any potential threat to Germany. The new Prague government was also anxious to avoid anything which might excite Berlin's displeasure. The significance of this new move by the dictator was the revelation that he didn't feel tied to any treaty and that he would use any advantages gained by extortion only as a starting-point for further extortion. Winston Churchill had seen through this strategy immediately after the signing of the Munich Agreement and characterised it with a striking illustration:

> One pound was demanded at the pistol's point. When it was given, two pounds were demanded at the pistol's point. Finally the dictator consented to take one pound seventeen and six and the rest in promises of goodwill for the future.[50]

In the years 1938 and 1939, as Hitler behaved with the greatest non chalance, he can have had no idea that in 1940 Stalin and Molotov would treat him in exactly the same way.

As a result of these bitter experiences, the illusions of the Western democracies concerning the success of 'appeasement' receded and finally disappeared. The mood of public opinion changed to one of revulsion. Insistent demands were made for more energetic action against the obviously insatiable dictator. In June 1939 a French public opinion poll showed that seventy-six per cent of the populace would favour opposing the Germans by force in the event of an armed aggression against Danzig.[51] Moreover, Chamberlain considered himself to have been personally hoodwinked by Hitler's advance into what was left of Czechoslovakia; the result (not achieved without some objections) was the British declaration guaranteeing support for Poland. Hitler countered on 28 April by revoking the Anglo–German naval agreement and the German–Polish non-aggression pact. This added more tension to the already critical political situation in Europe, which was being closely monitored by the Soviet Union.

The British Government's guarantee to Poland has been widely criticised because it made Britain dependent on an unpredictable partner, encouraged Warsaw to adopt an intransigent policy, and thus contributed towards the outbreak of war. By now the stage of concern about diplomatic blunders had long been passed. Hitler had demonstrated to the world, by the example of Czechoslovakia, that his victims had nothing to hope from subservience and a readiness to make concessions. If one agreed to his first 'moderate' demands, one had soon to reckon with new and far more excessive requirements. The leaders in Warsaw were, of course, well aware of the fact that the questions at issue were not merely Danzig, the admittedly difficult problem of the Polish Corridor, and the situation of the German minority. Much more was at stake – namely the independence and very existence of the Polish state. Incidentally, feelers had been sent out by the Germans regarding Polish entry into the Anti-Comintern Pact; but such ideas had little attraction for the Poles since it would inevitably mean that their country – as happened later to Hungary and Rumania – would degenerate into a German satellite state, and they would also risk being robbed of the fruits of a possible victory. Relying on the English guarantee, the Warsaw leaders therefore decided not to yield to German pressure, but to offer armed resistance if it came to the worst. In reaching this decision they considerably underestimated the striking force of the German Army.

The background to these events was the fate of countries belonging to the *cordon sanitaire*, the east and central European group of buffer states which Germany, and soon also Soviet Russia, was seeking to annex. The British and French did not wish to sacrifice these states, but could not protect them owing to the changing pattern of military power in the area. It became more and more obvious that their fate would be decided between Berlin and Moscow.

This problem was central to the negotiations between the Western powers and the Soviet Union which were carried out in the last months before the outbreak of war in an effort to frighten Hitler out of his new adventure. An agreement at this stage would have made the dictator realise the dangers of a war on two fronts against a superior coalition, and might have caused him to adopt a more moderate attitude. This would have meant not only saving the peace, but also preserving the integrity of the east and central European buffer states. However, Stalin was as little interested in this as Hitler. Furthermore, these negotiations were burdened with even more basic problems, which particularly concerned the British.

> On the one hand their policy was categorically based on peace and its preservation, the combined result of a deeply rooted aversion to war and the necessity, derived from self-interest, of avoiding a military conflict. On the other hand they believed that the Soviet Union was interested in provoking a war between the capitalist nations. British politicians were torn between their own desire for peace and the knowledge that the revolutionary aims of the Bolsheviks could only be furthered by a war in west and central Europe – from which the Soviet Union could arise like a phoenix from the ashes of a shattered European civilisation. As a result of such a war – in which the USSR would take no part – a communist Europe would fall like a ripe fruit into the lap of the Soviet rulers . . . this war was dreaded as a catalyst for the world revolution.[52]

A stable Europe, which might also include Hitler's Germany, seemed to many British politicians to be the best safeguard against these dangers.

But the gambler in the State Chancellery had no intention of subjecting Germany to such an inflexible arrangement, and thus – unwittingly to be sure – he became an instrument of Kremlin policy. It had been appreciated for some time in Moscow that good use could be made of Hitler's territorial aggression to cause the outbreak of the 'Second Imperialist War', and even at a time of mutual abuse, care was taken to avoid a complete rupture in relations with Berlin.[53] The Munich Agreement had averted an armed collision between Germany and the Western powers, but the clash seemed inevitable if Hitler was to adhere to the same policy. It was now a question of encouraging him in his expansionist intentions. Moscow therefore seized the initiative and made an approach to the 'deadly enemy'. In his speech at the XVIIIth Anniversary of the Communist Party on 10 March 1939 Stalin indicated that the Soviet Union had no desire for a conflict with Germany and emphasised

37

that his country was not willing to pull chestnuts out of the fire for other powers. This first signal was followed on 17 April – about the same time as the opening of the Moscow negotiations with England and France – by a visit to Secretary of State von Weizsäcker from Soviet Ambassador Merekalov, who strongly hinted that the relations between the two countries need not be prejudiced by their different ideologies. Shortly afterwards Molotov was appointed to replace the existing Foreign Minister Litvinov, who had supported a closer relationship with the Western powers and, being a Jew, had been less acceptable to the Germans as a negotiating partner. The new leader of Soviet foreign policy declared a little later that the recently discontinued economic negotiations with Germany could only be resumed if the necessary 'political basis' was established.

These soundings were received in Berlin with a certain interest, but also with caution and mistrust; no progress was made at first in either the political or the economic sphere, since the German negotiators suspected that the whole business was a Kremlin manoeuvre to exert pressure on the French and English. The Soviet leaders adopted a leisurely approach, however, for their position was being continually improved by the increasingly critical international situation and the growing tension between Germany and Poland. But when a German economic delegation visited London in July the Soviets were afraid that an agreement might be made which would frustrate their plans at the last moment. Meanwhile, Hitler's time was running out: he had planned the attack on Poland for the end of August and any significant delay would involve his forces in the difficulties of a winter campaign. As a result of these factors Berlin and Moscow soon came to terms.

In all this Stalin made brilliant use of his advantageous position. The time had come to encourage Hitler in his illusions and aggressive intentions and so unleash the war exactly according to the scenario already outlined by Lenin (see pages 14ff.). Everything soon worked out as planned. With the Soviet Union safely out of the equation, Hitler felt he could rest assured in his conviction that if he attacked Poland the Western Powers would yield without fighting, or limit themselves to a few diversionary actions. All warnings were in vain: the gambler had been so successful so often that nothing could shake his belief that he would win again.

However, this time things turned out differently. The dictator had made a false assessment of the resoluteness of the British statesmen in particular and of the general swing in public opinion in the West: the game was lost. The scene at the handing over of the English ultimatum on 3 September 1939 has been graphically portrayed by Paul Schmidt,

Hitler's chief interpreter at the time, in his well-known account of the proceedings:

> I stopped a short distance away in front of Hitler's table and then slowly translated for him the ultimatum of the British government. When I had finished, complete silence prevailed. Hitler remained sitting there as if petrified and stared into space. He didn't lose his temper, as was later asserted; he did not fly into a rage, as others have claimed. He kept sitting in his chair, completely quiet and not moving. After a while, which to me seemed an eternity, he turned to Ribbentrop, who was standing by the window, as if benumbed. 'What do we do now?' Hitler asked his Foreign Minister with a look of rage in his eyes, as if he wanted to make it clear that Ribbentrop had given him false information about the English. Ribbentrop replied in a quiet voice: 'I assume the French will hand over to us a similar ultimatum within the next hour.' . . . In the ante-room a deadly silence reigned at this announcement. Goering turned round to me and said: 'If we lose this war, then may heaven help us!' Goebbels stood in a corner, dejected and thoughtful, looking literally like the proverbial drenched poodle. Everywhere I saw disconsolate looks, even on the faces of the lesser Party officials who were in the room.[54]

Stalin's Dupe

'Now I have the world in my pocket!' Hitler is said to have exclaimed, bubbling with joy at the news of the conclusion of the treaty with the Kremlin.[55] This exclamation is not without a tinge of tragic and macabre irony, for the very situation which Max Weber (see page 18) had so urgently warned of had now occurred: if Germany made enemies of France and England at the same time, then Russia would have the nation in its pocket.

What this might have meant from Stalin's viewpoint may be demonstrated by considering the situation in the Soviet Union from a political and geostrategical point of view. In the course of the thirties a widening gap had opened between the 'imperialist' powers, between the aggressive and revisionist powers on the one hand, and the non-aggressive and satiated powers on the other. The former had united in the Anti-Comintern Pact against the Soviet Union and of these Germany and Japan were geographically close to the Soviet empire and could be considered as possible aggressors. This basically presented the danger of a war on two fronts, which could be especially threatening if those states could be used by the Western powers to spearhead an attack. Although the governments in London, Paris and Washington certainly had no such intentions, this possibility was attributed to them by Moscow, perhaps because of their intervention in the aftermath of the revolution. Whether such suspicions were genuinely harboured in the Kremlin must remain an open question, but in any case these possibilities could not be completely ignored. The Soviet leaders therefore considered it their first priority to guard against this danger by exploiting the considerable tensions and conflicts of interest between these two groups – playing them off against each other, and possibly involving them in a war. Working on these lines, Moscow might use Germany and Japan – Italy played a less important role – for an attack on the non-aggressive powers, who were in the long run the more dangerous, especially Britain and the U.S.A. Such a war would naturally shake the

40

capitalist world to its foundations and open up the possibility of revolutionary subversion in the centres of 'imperialism', and especially in the colonies. As well as the revolutionary possibilities there were military considerations: a direct attack on the maritime powers – England, Japan and America – was an impossibility because each of these nations had navies superior to the Red Fleet, which was also divided over four oceans and had no foreign bases. A situation could arise, however, in which the Red Army would be able to conquer the European continent, drive the Japanese back to their islands and, after excluding the British and Americans, control a continental bloc from Brittany to Kamchatka and Korea. This would naturally have repercussions in China and India and might eventually enable Moscow to become the dominant force in the Eurasian landmass, perhaps in the entire area of the ancient world.

Such expansionist ambitions were still far from being realised, but the Hitler–Stalin Pact, with its secret additional protocol, anticipated the division of the east European border states and allocated the lion's share of these to the Soviets. In their sphere of interest were Finland, Estonia, Latvia, Bessarabia and the Polish regions east of the line formed by the rivers Narev, Weichsel and San; Germany had to be satisfied with the parts lying to the west of that. Lithuania had at first been put into the German sphere of interest, but in the Boundaries and Friendship Agreement of 28 September it was exchanged for Lublin and the strip of land between the Weichsel and the Bug.

After the conclusion of this treaty Hitler and Ribbentrop may have regarded themselves as statesmen of the highest calibre; instead their actions betrayed a frightening lack of political intelligence. Whereas Stalin had thoroughly pondered over the content and phraseology of the agreements, his opposite numbers were obviously incapable even of carefully reviewing the consequences which might result for Germany from those fateful documents. In point of fact, the two treaties fitted in perfectly with Soviet long-term strategy, to involve Germany in a war with the British and the French, make it dependent on Russia and, if the opportunity should arise, bring about its extinction as an independent power. Far-sighted as he was, Stalin was already thinking at this early stage of obtaining a favourable starting point for the realisation of such plans. This was especially noticeable in provisions dealing with states on the Soviet Union's north and south flanks, where the conflict was to be started. By obtaining the allocation of Finland and the Baltic states, the Kremlin wanted not only to win back the position it had held in the days of the czarist empire as a great power in the Baltic, but also to gain a base from which the Red Fleet could at any time threaten the transport of Swedish ore to Germany. It was intended at the same time to lay hands on the important Finnish nickel mines and timber resources, and to take control of the agricultural production of the Baltic regions. In the south, annexation of Bessarabia would bring the Red Army threateningly nearer to the Rumanian oilfields, indispensable to Germany, and would signify at the same time a revival of the traditional Russian Balkan policy. Additionally, the Germans made a statement declaring their 'complete lack of interest' in the regions of south-east Europe, while the Kremlin made no mention at all of renouncing its aspirations in this area.

Moscow was also able to frame the agreement over Poland to accord with its own interests, as is clearly evidenced by the final positioning of the line of demarcation. The Germans did in fact receive the region between the Weichsel and the Bug; but in return they had to give up Lithuania, with its more valuable farmlands, and Ribbentrop's efforts to let Germany have the east Galician oilfield regions of Boryslav and Drohobics were unsuccessful. Furthermore, the course of the new line corresponded approximately to the Curzon Line, which the British had fixed in 1919 as the eastern border of Poland. In this way the Soviets could avoid offending the Western powers, but at the same time thrust the whole responsibility for the fate of the Poles on to Germany, and by so doing further prejudice Hitler's relations with England and France. In spite of this, the Soviet leaders retained for themselves – in the secret additional protocol – a voice in the final determination of Polish affairs. From the strategic point of view, the Kremlin also obtained important advantages. The Curzon Line (like the eastern border of today) had left the area around Bialystok in Poland, but the final demarcation line showed a remarkable deviation in this area, a bulge projecting into the west like a fist: this could hardly be explained as anything other than a deployment area for a possible attack. There was a similar kind of bulge, though even bigger, in east Galicia round Lemberg. This too was to play an important role in the Russian deployment of March 1941 (see page 106).

These facts reveal clearly enough that from the outset Stalin was concerned with keeping as firm a grip as possible on his German tool – from the economic, political and also, if need be, from the military point of view. Initially he had some success in this. How long and to what degree his supplies could protect his treaty partner from the effects of the British blockade now depended on him. By skilfully apportioning Soviet aid Stalin had it in his power to save Germany from defeat, but also to prevent them from achieving victory and so make the war drag on till both parties were exhausted, while the Soviet Union carried on rearming in safe neutrality in order to have the last word.

In the case of Poland Stalin's calculations worked out smoothly enough. In the eyes of the world – if not in the Soviet propaganda of the time – Germany had to bear the odium of the aggressor, as well as engage her armies in a bloody conflict, while Moscow kept quietly in the background, waited for the collapse of Polish resistance and then, without effort or risk, took possession of the eastern part of the state. Adhering closely to Lenin's precepts, Stalin used the utmost care to avoid making any real alliance with Germany – he did not wish to compromise himself too much in the eyes of the potentially more powerful opponents, the Western 'imperialists'.

Thus during the first weeks of 'co-operation' the cunning Georgian proved his superiority over the 'genius' of the Führer. While Hitler went storming at his victims like a mad bull, accompanied by an orchestration of ear-splitting propaganda, Stalin was, according to the excellent characterisation by George F. Kennan, a man of the greatest skill as far as political tactics and intrigue were concerned, a master not only in the choice of the right moment, but also in what Boris Nikolaievski has described as the art of dosing – doing things step by step and measuring out in every situation exactly how much he may allow himself; above all, Kennan suggests, in the art of playing people and forces off against each other for his own ends. In reality it was never he who struck with the knife, because he could always find others to carry out this business for him. He himself looked on at a distance, like a benevolent well-wisher; indeed, sometimes he even pretended to be annoyed or indignant. Stalin tried again and again to manipulate his opponents for his own ends, and readily finished them off when he had no more use for them. For example, he wanted to turn the nationalist forces in China against the English, American and Japanese, and intended to support them until they had fulfilled their task. Then they were to be annihilated, or, to use his own words, 'thrown aside like worn-out, wretched hacks'.[57]

It seems therefore quite possible that Stalin had already worked out how he intended to use Hitler's Germany when he got that country involved in a war with the Western powers. A similarly delicate manoeuvre had, admittedly, been unsuccessful in the case of Chiang Kai-shek; nor did the Führer let himself be too easily expedited to the knacker's yard. There are, however, important clues which suggest that during or shortly after the campaign in France the Georgian decided to liquidate his treaty partner, who had now become useless and potentially dangerous, and that he believed he could achieve the military superiority needed to do this (see pages 64 ff).

First of all, however, Stalin had to justify this pact with his former ideological enemy in the eyes of the public. One of his arguments was that the agreement was a blow against the Anti-Comintern Pact – an assertion apparently confirmed by restrained comments from Rome and indignant ones from Tokyo.[58] Another version stated that the 'fatherland of all workers' had been forced to sign the pact to avoid a war on two fronts: in evidence, reference was made to the fact that in the summer of 1939 serious fighting had broken out between Soviet and Japanese troops on the border between Manchuko and Outer Mongolia. With regard to the Far East, however, these reasons were not very convincing. A considerable part of the Japanese army had got bogged down in China and was incapable of a full-scale offensive against a new opponent as strong as the Soviet Union – as was finally indicated by their defeat at Chalchin Gol. In the west, however, there was no reason at all for such worries. It was repeatedly reported by the Soviets that the Western Powers, and especially the British, had given Hitler a 'free hand in the east' and even wanted to 'incite him to attack the Soviet Union'. In support of this claim the Kremlin pointed to the German–English economic negotiations – the so-called Wohltat Discussions – of July 1939. These were in reality aimed at a last-minute revival of the failed policies of appeasement by offering world-wide economic co-operation; but in return Germany would have to give up, as a matter of principle, all further aggressive actions.[59] Putting the matter somewhat crudely, the British had wanted to buy Hitler from his policy of expansion, something to which he would never have agreed. The attempt also failed when it was publicised because of the indignant reaction of English public opinion. After the experiences of Munich and Prague there was no longer any desire to be duped another time.[60] If the Wohltat Discussions caused some nervousness in Moscow, then it was mainly because a German–British agreement at this late date would have cut across Stalin's plans to incite Hitler to attack the West.[61]

Any sober judgement of the reaction of British politicians and public concludes that Hitler's march into Czechoslovakia sounded the death knell of appeasement and that the British guarantee to Poland could only be construed as a sign of Britain's resolute determination to oppose energetically any subsequent expansionist adventures on Hitler's part. From Stalin's point of view this guarantee also implied a guarantee for the Soviet Union's western border; and it was well known in Moscow that London was particularly anxious to prevent the establishment of a German continental empire. It is an open question whether the Kremlin was also aware that at the time Germany had neither the military means nor any operational plans for an attack on Russia. Viewed broadly, the thesis that England wanted to set Germany against Russia can only be regarded as an example of Moscow's familiar tactic of concealing its own intentions by attributing them to other powers. In this case – just as in the case of the assertion that Stalin made his pact with Hitler, with its dire consequences, through fear of a war on two fronts – it seems to be an unconvincing attempt to cover up the Kremlin's decisive share in the blame for unleashing the Second World War.[62]

Stalin's perceptive and sure-footed tactics had placed the Soviet Union in a strong position, but in the case of Germany the very opposite applied. Hitler was fully aware of this at the handing over of the British ultimatum when he asked the anxious question 'What now?' In itself, the subjection of Poland would present no great problem, especially after the pact with Russia. The German General Staff could exploit the semi-circular border line of the Polish state, running from eastern Prussia to Czechoslovakia; the defenders, on the other hand, had no comparable forces with which to oppose German air power and motorised units. Furthermore, the Polish General Staff completely misread the situation and concentrated its troops in the Corridor and the Posen area, thus exposing them to encirclement by the German Army.

For Hitler the contingency that the war against Poland might not be localised was wrapped in the mists of uncertainty. In September 1939 a plan of operations against the Allies didn't even exist; it had then to be hastily improvised.[63] There was no trace of a composite plan, embracing policy and strategy for a large-scale European or even a world war. As revealed in the documents covering the Führer's discussions on the subject, his response to the issues raised was completely immature, confused and superficial – especially by comparison with the writings of General Beck on the same period. For example, the report of a meeting on 23 May about the Polish problem states:

> It will come to a battle. Our task is to isolate Poland. The decisive factor is that isolation must succeed . . . we mustn't get involved at the same time in a conflict with the West.

But immediately after this is the statement:

> It is not certain that a war with the West can be avoided in the wake of a German–Polish confrontation; the struggle would then be first and foremost against England and France.[64]

This example gives a good illustration of the political–strategical think

45

ing of a man who has been called the 'greatest general of all times'. If Hitler was convinced that the attack on Poland could only succeed if that country were isolated from the West, then he should not have gone ahead with the invasion if this condition could not be met. Yet in the same breath his thoughts swing towards a war with the West. By contemplating this, after having got rid of military leaders who were very much aware of their responsibilities, Hitler was making an amateurish gamble with the destiny of Germany.

The same might be said of the treaty with Russia. The expression 'sphere of interest' was vague enough for Moscow to interpret according to its own ends – namely, the annexation and Sovietisation of the regions in question. Moscow had been given the right to express opinions on the future structure of the Polish area, and the formulation of the article on south-east Europe was even open to the interpretation that Germany had given up any political interests there. Moreover, the agreement had considerably improved the strategic, military and economic position of the Soviet Union compared with that of Germany, and procured for them a powerful basis from which to apply economic and military pressure. This would be made clear enough during Molotov's visit to Berlin.

Quite apart from this the German economy – owing to the maritime blockade – was largely dependent on imports from or via the Soviet Union. Although the autocratic policy of the pre-war years had certainly achieved some success,

> ... even in the textile branch the dependence on imports could only be cut down from ninety-five to about thirty-five per cent by 1939. The 'fat gap' was still there, with imports of forty-three per cent. In spite of the annexation of Austria and the erection of the *Reichswerke*, and also taking into consideration the inland scrap iron supplies, forty-five per cent of the iron ore needed still had to be imported. Likewise, after allowing for the conversion of used material, the dependence on foreign supplies amounted in 1939 to twenty-five per cent in zinc, fifty per cent in lead, seventy per cent in copper, ninety per cent in tin, ninety-five per cent in nickel, ninety-nine per cent in bauxite, sixty-six per cent in mineral oils, and eighty per cent in rubber.[65]

This shortfall could only partially be met by other European countries. The remainder had to be sought with the help of the Soviet Union, and in fact there was a considerable flow of goods from the east into Germany. In this way most of the bottlenecks in the raw-materials section of the German war economy could be cleared, but only at the price of dependence on the goodwill of Moscow.[66]

The Kremlin knew how to exploit this dependence with great consistency:

> Always, when it was a question of strengthening Hitler's will to wage war, Stalin delivered willingly and in great quantities. This was the case before, during and after the Polish campaign, and again in October 1939 when it helped prevent a possible agreement between Hitler and England. The same tendency was apparent at the beginning and end of the campaign in the west. In the first days of the German offensive support for Germany was based on the well-known miscalculation that Germany was the weaker of the two opponents. At the conclusion of the operation the top priority was to convince Hitler that it was not necessary to make any concrete offers of peace to London. Always at a time when Russia had difficulties in the Baltic area and an intervention by the Western powers seemed possible – as during the Russo–Finnish War and the German Operation Weserübung [the attack on Denmark and Norway] – the Kremlin cut down its supplies, which thus became a formidable weapon in the Soviet political armoury.[67]

By rationing the provision of supplies as and when he saw fit, Stalin could use Germany, as he had planned to, against his real enemies, the Western powers, while avoiding any direct confrontation with them.

Another aspect of German–Soviet trade relations at the time is worthy of mention. While Moscow delivered almost exclusively raw materials to its partner, the Soviets demanded – and for the most part received – armaments and industrial equipment in return. This enabled Soviet experts to gain completely legal access to German armament factories and so establish some idea of their capacity. They were thus able to make comparisons – which often enough confirmed their favourable impression of their own country's war potential. The Soviet interest in the German navy was such that they asked for construction plans of the battleship *Bismarck* – additional evidence that Moscow considered the Western sea powers to be its real opponents.

Looking back over the history of these events it seems quite incomprehensible that the Führer allowed himself to become dependent on such a dangerous opponent.[68] But in this case he was not dealing, as hitherto, with intimidated bourgeois politicians, full of moral scruples, but with an opponent who was at least his match in ruthlessness and far superior in cunning. During the negotiations and settlement of the fateful Moscow agreements, the Bohemian-like dilettante Hitler and the vain braggart Ribbentrop displayed astonishing frivolity and a staggering lack of political intelligence, and so played into the hands of the master of the Soviet empire.

In their high-risk game Hitler and his foreign minister were obviously staking everything on one card: namely, that during the attack on

Poland the Western powers would once again remain quiet and the Soviets would be satisfied with their gains from the agreements with Germany. However, if things turned out otherwise exceedingly dangerous consequences must result. And of course things really did turn out otherwise. When England and France declared war Stalin had Hitler in his pocket and was the arbiter of all Europe.

With Poland out of the reckoning the dreaded war on two fronts had been avoided for the time being, but England and France were beginning to mobilise their far greater resources, with the U.S.A. backing them up, and Hitler could be under no illusions as to the loyalty of his eastern treaty partner. If he ran into difficulties in his confrontation with the Western powers he had to be ready for any eventuality from Moscow. He had not the means to overcome the British, with their mastery of the seas; he could merely hope that military assaults might force them to seek or come to some other arrangement. This would open up the possibility of attacking the Soviet Union and defeating it in a battle between two land powers, but Hitler underestimated the resoluteness as well as the military potential of the eastern Empire.

At this stage Hitler realised that he had become involved in a critical situation and that time was working against him,[69] and for this reason he would have been willing to conclude a peace treaty which ensured that he kept his Polish booty. In accordance with this, and in the framework of the Border and Friendship Treaty of 28 September 1939, a joint German–Soviet declaration was made which expressed the following point of view:

> . . . that it would serve the true interests of all people, to put an end to the state of war existing between Germany on the one hand, and England and France on the other. The two governments will therefore direct their joint efforts to achieve this goal as soon as possible. If, however, the efforts of the two governments remain unsuccessful, this would emphasise the fact that England and France are responsible for the continuance of the war.[70]

The next day *Pravda* made the following commentary:

> The situation is clear: it depends solely on the English and French governments whether this war, started against the will of the people, is to be continued – a war which threatens the whole world with renewed carnage. If the efforts of the Russian and German governments are without result, then it is certain that England and France, their governments and ruling classes, are responsible for the continuation of the war.[71]

In a speech on 6 October 1939 Hitler also made a personal appeal for peace to the Western powers, which was immediately rejected.

Stalin certainly had no desire to end the war he had so skilfully engineered, but he assumed correctly that the call for peace would be rejected and used the opportunity to lay the blame for the war on the Western powers and put on record his own love of peace. Even if hostilities had ceased, against all expectations, the Soviets would have been able to play an authoritiative role at a general peace conference and probably win international ratification of their territorial gains.

Soon after the conquest of eastern Poland, Moscow began to take possession of its 'sphere of interest' in the Baltic area, as allocated in the treaty. In a framework of 'assistance pacts' the Baltic states were compelled to allow Soviet military bases on their territories. In so doing, the Soviets declared that they would respect the political, economic and social structure of these lands; this certainly did not, however, prevent them being annexed and undergoing Sovietisation in the summer of 1940. It was intended to impose a similar pact on the Finns, but they refused to yield to extortion. The result was the Winter War of 1939–40, which created for all interested parties a complex and delicate situation. It could hardly be a matter of indifference to Germany if the Finnish nickel mines and timber resources, important for military purposes, fell into the hands of the Russians, but Hitler and Ribbentrop had handed Finland over to Moscow by the treaty. The Western powers, giving as their reason the need to provide help for Finland, seized this opportunity to establish themselves in the far north, occupy the areas of the ore mines, and so obtain a position on the flank against both Germany and Russia. Soviet intervention would have been inopportune because of the danger of a direct confrontation with England and France, which Stalin wanted to avoid at all costs.

The Finns defended themselves with the utmost bravery and skill, inflicting heavy losses on the attackers. Serious faults in the training and tactics of the Red Army were revealed, which seemed to justify the contempt in which Soviet forces were held – opinions shared by the general staffs of both Germany and the Western powers. The first phase of the war ended in dismal failure for the Soviet Union. Nevertheless, a reorganisation, energetically carried out by Marshal Timoschenko, allowed the larger Soviet forces to win substantial victories and the Finns had to thank Stalin's respect for the Western powers that, temporarily at least, they could maintain their independence, even though they suffered painful losses. This situation could quickly change, however, if this respect for the Western powers was no longer necessary, as soon proved to be the case. Once again the Germans did the Russians an extremely valuable service when in April 1940 they landed in Norway and so eliminated an Allied threat from the north. The success of this bold venture, which cost the weak German naval forces heavy losses, was decisively assisted by hesitation on the part of the Norwegians, which had dire consequences. The Norwegian government, informed several days in advance of the planned attack,[72] failed to decide on a general mobilisation, in spite of urgent admonitions by the Chief of the General Staff. If this had been done promptly the German enterprise would probably have ended in failure.[73] Although Moscow had not been forewarned of the action – a clear breach of the terms of the Hitler–Stalin Pact – the Kremlin made no protests. The campaign in Norway meant more to Stalin than a clarification of the position in Scandinavia: it meant that for the first time major actions were being fought out between Germany and the Allies. The Phoney War began to show great promise of developing into a real 'imperialist' war.

Soviet anxieties regarding the Western powers were by no means imaginary. Leaders in London and Paris were considering how they could take military measures against the Soviets, who were considered to be allies of Germany. Besides contemplating actions in the north, consideration was also given to bombing the oilfields of Baku, or even sending land forces into the Caucasus, possibly with the co-operation of Turkish or Iranian troops. There were, however, considerable differences of opinion between the English and the French, so that the ideas put forward never produced any concrete preparations. On the whole, these proposals might be regarded as expressions of embarrassment;[74] besides, the Allies soon had other worries.

The German invasion of France finally created the situation Stalin had been hoping for. The 'imperialist' war had now broken out in all its violence. Accordingly, Moscow at first lent Germany increased moral and material support. In the Kremlin it was at first expected that there would be long-drawn-out battles with a heavy rate of attrition – as in the First World War – in the course of which the two sides would go on destroying each other until general exhaustion brought about a revolutionary situation. Instead of this the German army achieved, in a matter of weeks, a victory which was as brilliant as it was unexpected. This success was mainly due to the adoption of military tactics which were far in advance of their opponents'; but here too Hitler was helped by serious, indeed scarcely comprehensible, mistakes on the part of the Allies. The German intention of thrusting forwards through the Ardennes towards the English Channel and encircling the Allied forces to the north of this wedge had been known in the West for some considerable time. On 8 March, at a discussion about the situation, King Leopold of Belgium made an assessment which was in most parts correct and passed it on to the French[75] – who took no action and made no deductions from the information. Without incurring any risks, the

French could have sent a dozen divisions, elite units standing unused behind the Maginot Line amongst them, to cover the hinge of their deployment. Even the Belgians failed to send reinforcements to their troops in the Ardennes; the main body of their forces remained in the north, where it was sacrificed to encirclement and destruction. Thus the German army was able celebrate a great victory with astonishingly light losses. The French were as good as eliminated as a military force and as a factor in power politics. The British, having been driven from the continent with the loss of almost all their military equipment, would for years be unable to engage in any large-scale operations on the continent, even with the possible help of the Americans. The triumph in the West did, however, signify the turning point in the Soviet policy for Germany. The Moor had served his purpose.

Power Politics and Ideology

It cannot be exactly determined to what extent the French collapse was caused by communist propaganda, subversion and sabotage. It is, however, true that under the banner of the Hitler–Stalin Pact not only the Soviet Union as a state but also the Comintern worked against the Western powers, admittedly without identifying themselves with Germany or giving up completely their subversive activities in that country. On the instructions of their Moscow masters the French communists were active in opposing their country's war efforts, even going so far as to collaborate with Hitler's secret service.

On the whole, France offers an impressive example of the ideological and propagandist strategies of the Kremlin. After the First World War it was considered to be the strongest 'imperialist' military power, and communist activists used all possible psychological and political means to undermine its defence capabilities – especially since during the intervention in the Soviet Union French troops had proved to be anything but immune to the influence of propaganda. For a long time, therefore, the Party line was that of 'revolutionary defeatism', and even after Hitler seized power this line remained in force relatively unchanged. When two years' national service was introduced as a result of Germany's rearming, this was bitterly opposed by the communists. In the spring of 1935 the Party leader Maurice Thorez declared: 'We will never allow the working classes to be driven into a so-called defensive war of democracy against Fascism.'[76] A few weeks later a contradictory order came from Moscow, where in the meantime a decision had been made in favour of the concept of a 'Popular Front' and the 'common struggle of all democrats against the fascist enemies of mankind'. In spite of serious doubts on the part of the non-communist parties of the left, this united front was soon established. The Spanish Civil War intensified the polarity between right and left, and when the bourgeois governments of England and France finally capitulated at Munich, the communists could rightfully step in and declare themselves to be the only true and uncompro

52

mising anti-fascist party. Anything with the semblance of an agreement with Hitler was furiously attacked. As late as 6 August 1939, for example, the prominent communist politician Gabriel Péri wrote in the main organ of his party, after his return from a conference in London:

> Everyone believes that the alliance between France and England is an essential factor in the defence of international peace and in resistance to the atrocities of fascism. With our friends in the English parliament, we have decided to urge the common people in our two countries to co-operate in this policy of a joint defence of democracy.[77]

Following this line of thought even the communist delegates voted with their bourgeois and socialist colleagues on 2 September 1939 for the introduction of war credits. Yet after Hitlerite fascism had been fought against for years as the number one enemy of humanity, the 'fatherland of all workers' had now made a pact with these satanic powers. This news, which broke on 23 August, fell like a bombshell, affecting not only communists in France, who were extremely confused and bewildered, but also dumbfounding those who had risked their lives and their health in the Spanish Civil War or in street battles with militant right-wing radicals. Communist leaders, who struggled to make comprehensible to themselves and to the people of the Party something which seemed quite incomprehensible, suffered acute embarrassment. As Moscow was silent at first, there were numerous attempts to explain the situation, which often contradicted each other. A widely-held theory was that in making this treaty the Soviet Union wanted to destroy the Anti-Comintern Pact and so save the peace; if in spite of that it came to war, then the communists, together with the united French people, had to carry out their duty. This line was firmly adhered to even in the first weeks after the outbreak of war, and the resistance of the Poles to the German invasion was accordingly highly praised.

However, when the Red Army marched into eastern Poland the situation changed completely. This move by the Russians caused the greatest indignation in France – even in ultra-left socialist circles, where it was regarded as open complicity with the fascist policy of conquest. But at the same time the communists at last received clear instructions from Moscow, involving a complete change of tack. The Kremlin ordered its followers to work against the war efforts of their country and support Hitler's Germany, at least indirectly. This was too much to swallow for many communists, including prominent Party members, who resigned and frequently gave reasons for their decision in public declarations. Vital Gayman, for instance, who had been general secretary of the Party newspaper *L'Humanité* and had fought in

Spain as a high-ranking officer, was no left-wing intellectual sympathiser but a veteran of the Party. He wrote on 6 October:

> However complex the interests of the class or the nation which are now at stake in this present war may be, one thing is certain: the interests of the people cannot be defended or represented by the same camp in which are found the executioners of the German people, the murderers of the Spanish people, the destroyers of the freedom of the Austrian and Czech peoples and the invaders of Poland. I am convinced that I would betray the legacy of my comrades in arms, who have fallen on Spanish soil in the struggle against the fascism of Franco, Mussolini and Hitler, if I omitted to declare most emphatically my total rejection of a policy which is pursuing a goal diametrically opposed to the one for which, generously and heroically, they have sacrificed their lives.[78]

However, the protests and resignations of anti-fascists achieved nothing at all. The main body of the Party obeyed the new orders with their customary allegiance.

It is a depressing fact that anti-fascist fighters in the Spanish Civil War often met with a grim fate in the Soviet Union. Many of them were liquidated or put into camps; others disappeared without trace or died suddenly an unexplained death. Zealous Marxist beliefs, a revolutionary readiness for self-sacrifice and enthusiasm for the working class were obviously viewed with suspicion by the despot in the Kremlin. What he needed was bureaucratic submissiveness and slavish obedience.

The main purpose of 'the anti-fascist solidarity of all democracies' had been to prevent a rapprochement between Hitler and the Western powers. When war was declared this goal had been achieved; furthermore, the Kremlin now supported Germany for reasons of power politics – Hitler's forces could be used as a battering ram against the 'imperialists'. Anti-fascism had served its purpose and now – at least for the time being – it was finished.

It was perfectly obvious at the time that the main thrust of Soviet policy was directed at the Western powers: this was true before, during and after the Second World War. The anti-Hitler coalition which came later did not alter this fact but, very much to Moscow's advantage, veiled it from the eyes of democratic politicians and public opinion in the Western countries.

In all this the Kremlin made no efforts to hide its attitude. On 31 October Molotov attacked the Western Allies more bitterly than ever before. In a speech to the Supreme Soviet he stated that:

> . . . the British Government have proclaimed that the war against Germany is aimed at nothing more or less than the destruction of Hitlerism.

This means that both in England and France the advocates of the war against Germany have declared a kind of ideological war, in the manner of the old religious crusades. The National Socialist ideology, as indeed any other, can be supported or rejected, but everyone understands that an ideology cannot be destroyed by force, so it is senseless and even criminal to wage such a war to destroy Hitlerism by cloaking this conflict in the mantle of the struggle for democracy.[79]

With this speech Molotov was also giving a lead to French communism. Whereas a short time previously the battlecry had been for the solidarity of all democracies against fascism, the enemy of mankind, now the ideological war was condemned as senseless and criminal. The Germans made prompt use of this comradely help and threw down over France leaflets quoting the relevant passages of Molotov's speech. An agitation against the 'imperialist war' was immediately started, aimed less at peace than at demoralising the French people and the French army. Although by this time the Communist Party and its press had been prohibited, their parliamentary representatives carried on working under the title 'French Workers' and Peasants' Group'. In a letter to the president of the Chamber of Deputies, this group demanded an immediate public debate about the already mentioned (see page 46) Russo–German peace initiative; the writers made a significant distinction between Hitler's Germany and the 'imperialist warmongers' – in other words the governments of Britain and France. Léon Blum, the former head of the Popular Front government, wrote a few days later that reading this document had almost made him vomit: 'Dispensed in such doses, cynicism and hypocrisy are physically unbearable.'[80]

Communist activity soon swung completely in the direction of 'revolutionary defeatism'. The Party began to build up an underground organisation and initiate various subversive activities. For example, an illegal leaflet entitled 'Letter to the French Soldiers' urged . . .

> the forces of peace to get together immediately in order to prevent the unleashing over you, in a matter of weeks or months, of the deafening noise of bloody battles and over your families an iron rain and the fire of bombardments.[81]

Incitements to sabotage were also made. One leaflet stated:

> Workers, don't be the accomplices of your worst enemies, who are fighting against the triumph in the Soviet Union of socialism over one sixth of the earth's surface; hinder and delay war production: make these products unusable, with all suitable means, employing all the powers of your mind and all your technical knowledge.[82]

Although this pamphlet was aimed directly against arms deliveries to Finland in the aftermath of the Russian attack, it applied also to the whole of the French arms industry. There were, in fact, fairly frequent acts of sabotage, causing damage to parked vehicles and other products, especially in tank and aircraft factories. Armoured vehicles and aircraft were weapons of decisive importance, so it can be assumed that such acts of sabotage were made by persons with a degree of technical knowledge.

The French government sought to reduce sabotage by conscription, but this led to an increase in communist agitation within the armed forces, which took on ever more aggressive forms. The illegally published *Humanité*, for example, reported on 10 April 1940:

> The men and women workers . . . the soldiers, destined to be massacred because of Swedish iron or Rumanian oil, are not afraid of death! They prefer to risk death in the struggle to end the capitalist regimes of war and misery than to die for the big industrialists.[83]

This was a scarcely concealed summons to revolt and mutiny.

It has also become known that there was collaboration between the French communists and the German secret police. Soon after the commencement of hostilities the German intelligence services began to establish connections, especially through Belgium, with Communist Party members and functionaries,

> . . . in order to distribute in France defeatist and anti-British leaflets. Together with this, the communist agents were also given directions and technical instructions on methods of sabotaging the French arms industry.[84]

During the campaign in the west the Germans found out that the demoralising leaflets really had found their way into the hands of the troops. When General de Gaulle carried on with the struggle from England after the capitulation of France, the German secret service

> . . . put a 'Special Staff H' into operation, with the task of maintaining contact with the French communists, but using different phraseology. This was directed against de Gaulle, who was portrayed as a mere mercenary of Western capitalism, and against the reactionary British ally, who had ignominiously left the French in the lurch.[85]

Hitler had indeed used peace propaganda much earlier to cripple the French will to resist. This peace offensive is portrayed in masterly fashion by Wilhelm von Schramm in his book *Speak of Peace If You*

Want War.[86] This shows how, with demagogic cunning and for his own insidious ends, Hitler managed to exploit the idealism of many who genuinely sought an understanding between the two nations – amongst them numerous intellectuals and especially members of the French war veterans' associations – without them even noticing how their honest intentions were being abused. Even General Ludwig Beck, a declared opponent of the adventurous policies to assassinate Hitler, unwittingly assisted in this deception. The use of the peace offensive as an instrument of psychological warfare was thus employed against the French people by both Hitler and Stalin, though in different ways and with different ends in mind.

The Communist International was also active in other nations, using every means at its disposal to weaken resistance to Hitler's policy of conquest,[87] which it had so recently condemned as fascist aggression. It agitated in the United States against any support for the English and French and promoted similar activities in England itself. For example, on 3 October 1939 the Communist Member of Parliament Gallacher demanded in the House of Commons that peace negotiations be opened immediately; indeed, in January 1940 the Party even managed to call together a 'People's Congress', which criticised the 'imperialist war' and the patriotic attitude of the Labour Party. The extent to which homage was paid to the doctrine of revolutionary defeatism was described by, amongst others, the prominent communist Douglas Hyde, after his break with the Party. He wrote about the defeat which Hitler's army had inflicted on the Western powers in the spring of 1940:

> As communists we had a very understandable interest in defeats. The October revolution of 1917 was the result of a military defeat, as were the workers' and soldiers' councils of the Germany of 1918 and the Hungarian Soviets. We had more to gain from a defeat than from a victory.[88]

When it was a question of weakening the position of the Western powers, ideological differences had no role to play. When, for example, the Belgian Rexist Movement – which sympathised with fascism – opposed all concessions to England and France it was congratulated on this attitude by the organ of the Communist Party, *Le Monde*, in its issue of 7 October 1939.[89] Incidentally, the Rexist leader Léon Degrelle later held a high rank in the Waffen SS, and founded the Walloon Legion which fought on the German side against the Soviet Union.

When the German offensive was started on 10 May 1940 the French communists had no intention of calling for their country to be defended against the fascist aggression – in the way the Jacobins of revolutionary France had appealed to the nation to defend itself against invasion by conservative powers. On the contrary, they condemned the governments of the capitalist and imperialistic warmongers in more and more strident terms, demanded exemplary punishment for these, and campaigned for an immediate peace. On 17 May the leading article of *Humanité* summoned its readers to fight for

> a government of peace, which is rooted in the mass of the people and takes measures against reaction, a government which comes to an immediate agreement with the Soviet Union to restore world peace.[90]

It is not quite clear what conception of the future lay behind this agitation. Probably those advocating it had in mind revolutionary uprisings which would lead to a 'people's democratic government' under Maurice Thorez. It might have been hoped that the Germans, on the basis of the pact with Stalin, would at least tolerate such a government; perhaps the worker in his German army uniform might even fraternise with his French counterpart. There was, however, no revolution. The exhausted populace wanted order to be re-established and an economy which functioned reasonably well. The new French government in Vichy was even more anti-communist than its predecessor and the German army was practically immune to all attempts to infiltrate it. Above all, Hitler considered the demarcation of spheres of interest agreed upon with the Soviets as final, and wouldn't have been willing to tolerate a communist centre of power in the West. Whether the Kremlin was considering the possibility of getting a firm grip on Germany and Italy by means of a people's democracy in France is doubtful.

In any case, even after peace was declared the French communists sought – for reasons of their own – to get on friendly terms with the victors. In so doing they could point to the fact that they alone had supported the German–Russian peace campaign, that they had worked to weaken the French will to resist and that they were now opposing the continuation of the war in the colonies. For their part the Germans needed a rapid resumption of work in the factories, and communist help would be very welcome. In return the Party demanded the liberation and rehabilitation of communist deputies and activists 'who had been imprisoned because they fought for peace'; they also wanted 'all those who involved France in the war and deceived the French people in order to carry out their criminal policies [in other words those who had opposed Hitler's aggression] to be publicly prosecuted and sentenced.'[91] In addition, the confiscation of all war profits and massive taxation of all excess wealth was called for, together with a comprehensive programme of nationalisation. Above all, the Party should be granted legal status once more. However, some of these demands were not met – either because of objections from the Vichy government or because of mistrust on the part the upper echelons of the Wehrmacht. For a while, then, the communists had to be satisfied with a kind of semi-legal status, but they refrained from conflict with the occupying power. Their criticisms did not fully emerge until the increase in tension (especially in the Balkans) between Germany and the Soviet Union in the spring of 1941.

But 22 June marked a significant turning point in events. By Hitler's invasion of France the 'fatherland of all workers' was directly endangered. England – until recently condemned as plutocratic, capitalist and imperialist – became an ally overnight, and once again – as before the Hitler–Stalin Pact – the banners proclaimed the solidarity of all democracies against the fascist enemies of mankind. In union with de Gaulle – recently reviled as the mercenary slave of British supercapitalism – appeals were made to the patriotic sentiments of the French, and attempts were even made to excel the general in this. At first the communists had simply joined the Resistance; now they tried to take over the reins of leadership and elbow out the other groups in order to be ready to seize power when the war ended. Although this goal was to remain unattainable, they did succeed in passing themselves off as patriotic freedom fighters risking their all for a brighter future, and thus gained an enormous increase in prestige. Artists and intellectuals in particular found it fashionable to join the Party or to show sympathy for it.

All this led, of course, to extraordinary paradoxes. Under the banner of the Hitler–Stalin Pact the communists had condemned the ideological war as senseless and criminal, but now, as if nothing had happened, they professed once more to be the only true and irreconcilable anti-fascists. A short time before, obedient to the doctrine of revolutionary defeatism, they had sabotaged the defence efforts of the French, collaborated with the Germans and demanded the heads of capitalist warmongers. Now they strutted and proclaimed themselves to be the country's true patriots and demanded the heads of the collaborators. It is remarkable that this sickening volte-face, worthy of the Vicar of Bray, scarcely affected the popularity of the Party – a dauntingly successful piece of cool speculation as to the short memory of humanity in general and those 'intellectuals' in particular on whose 'intelligence', as is well known, the gods themselves make war in vain.

Acting on instructions from Moscow, French communists had made three 180-degree turns from revolutionary defeatism to anti-fascism in the six years between 1935 and 1941. These manoeuvres were all carried out purely for reasons of power politics; nonetheless, some ideological justification had to be found, and in each case the 'scientific' wonder weapon of Marxism, dialectics, was ready and waiting. An article written in 1943 by Party ideologist Etienne Fajon, which treats the phases of communist policy since 1934 'in the light of dialectics', concluded with the concise formula: 'Since the time of Galileo we have known that science is always victorious. Communist policy is a science. It will succeed.'[92]

The real truth concerning the alleged scientific character of dialectics was uncovered long ago: it is all about a number of empty formulae and other devices which allow all kinds of assertions to be protected against any contradiction based on logical rules or hard facts, and which enable any kind of political regulation or decision to acquire surreptitiously the semblance of a higher justification. In any case, the dialectician is 'infallible'.[93] These are no 'bourgeois' insinuations. The master himself revealed in a little known passage that he knew very well the usefulness of dialectics in this connection and employed it quite intentionally. In a letter to Engels dated 15 August 1857 and not intended for publication, Marx tells of an article which he had written for the *New York Daily Tribune* about a revolt in India. Unfortunately, the military situation there did not develop at all as he had expected. But that was no reason for being disconcerted for, Marx added – perhaps with a prophetic smile –

> . . . it is possible I've made a fool of myself, but that can always be remedied with a little bit of dialectics. I've framed my assertions in such a manner that I'll still be right even if the reverse takes place.[94]

The dialectician is always right. Stalin knew that of course, but he didn't restrict himself to the Marxist repertoire. When it seemed useful to him, he employed pan-Slavonic and even sometimes pan-Orthodox ideas. At the signing of the Friendship Treaty with Belgrade on 6 April 1941, for instance, he said to the Yugoslavian Ambassador Gavrilovic:

> 'We are brothers of the same blood and the same religion. Nothing can separate our two countries from each other. I hope that your army can hold up the Germans for a long time' . . . [After the signing] Stalin went up to Gavrilovic, gave him a hearty handshake and then, before turning away, made the sign of the cross in the pravo-Slavonic manner, with the right hand after the left as is the custom with the Russians and the Serbs, as if he wanted to bless the Yugoslav minister.[95]

Mikojan, who was present at this scene, had to put a handkerchief before his mouth to avoid bursting out into loud laughter.

Stalin was also skilled at conjuring up an appearance of democracy, something he did with astonishing success when he wanted to deceive and manipulate Western democrats. In such matters he often displayed great generosity: for example, during the period of popular front politics and rapprochement with the West he provided the Soviet state with a perfect democratic facade in the form of a constitution which embraced every possible right and freedom. All had the right to vote from the age of eighteen; there were free, secret and direct elections in various state and communal Soviet institutions, a two-chamber parliament, together with freedom of speech, the press and religious worship. After the Soviet Union joined the League of Nations there was a swing in foreign policy towards detente and the idea of collective security. By this means the Soviet Union was gradually to appear

> . . . in the eyes of the public in England and America as a democratic state almost comparable with those of Great Britain and France, and moreover as an ardent campaigner for peace, disarmament and collective security; also as a convinced opponent of the aggressive plans of the fascist states and as an unselfish protector of the freedom and independence of the small nations. Finally, the Soviet Union was to be the only great power to keep on trying, without any selfish or ulterior motives, to realise in political practice the high principles for which the League of Nations was allegedly fighting.[96]

Behind this facade, however, enforced industrialisation and rearmament was continuing, mass terror took on ever more frightful forms and the 'Gulag Archipelago' became populated with countless victims. The actual purpose of hoodwinking the world outside was, and remained, to prevent a rapprochement between Germany and the Western democracies and so to prepare the ground for the 'second imperialistic war'.

Nevertheless, this myth of the 'peace-loving and democratic Soviet Union', created by Stalin with cold-blooded aplomb, achieved considerable success in impressing public opinion in the West. Particularly in left-wing circles, it took on the character of a religious belief which could not be shaken by logical arguments. In such circles all political news items from Soviet sources were considered to be absolutely reliable. To express any doubt at all as to the truth of their contents was considered to be inappropriate and had, as these left-wing intellectuals asserted,

> . . . its roots in reactionary prejudices or a failure to understand the 'signs of the times'. The utterance of critical remarks about the Soviet Union was all the more objectionable because it was interpreted as a sign of sympathy for Nazi Germany.[97]

61

These intellectual circles certainly did not occupy the key positions of power, especially in England, but they could influence the cultural climate and public opinion, and thus indirectly influence policy. In fact, Moscow achieved only a partial success, for influential conservative groups regarded the popular front with the deepest mistrust, and even amongst left-wing intellectuals many doubts began to creep in because of the Stalinist rule of terror. Yet even then the Soviet dictator realised how vulnerable the democracies were to skilfully conducted propaganda and psychological warfare, and how much pressure he could exert if he succeeded in imbuing public opinion with a political myth advantageous to himself; for this reason such a myth can, under the right circumstances, be worth more than dozens of divisions.

At a decisive stage in the Second World War Stalin was to launch an even more effective myth – that of the 'malicious and treacherous attack of the fascist aggressors on the unsuspecting and peace-loving Soviet Union'.

The Moor Has Served His Purpose

> Like a new Napoleon, Hitler is running amok throughout Europe, conquering great countries, terrifying the placid bourgeoisie. All this seems very heroic to him and his party members. The Nazis see the dawning of a new Middle Ages with themselves and Duke Adolf at centre stage. This vision of the future will also turn out to be a 'misunderstanding'. When the work is done, the conqueror of the world, with his fellow criminals, will end up where he belongs – on the rubbish heap of world history. The Moor has served his purpose. The Moor can go.

This extract appeared in an essay in the July 1940 number of the Comintern journal *The Red Dawn*, published in the Soviet Union.[98] The remarkable thing is not only the open, indeed crude, criticism of the German head of state, but also the implication of the last sentences, especially when these are related to utterances made by Stalin himself on a similar theme. As already mentioned (page 43), Stalin hoped to use the bourgeois–nationalist forces in China as a tool against the foreign 'imperialists', and then to 'throw them aside, like worn-out, wretched hacks'. On another occasion he said of Chiang Kai-shek and his followers: 'We must make use of them and cannot throw the lemon away until it is squeezed dry.'[99] By his victory in the west Hitler had, in fact, achieved all he could for Soviet interests, and further advantages were not to be expected from him. The Moor had served his purpose, and could now be dumped.

Such considerations have so far scarcely been acknowledged in current historical research; yet now more than ever we seem to be in a position to elucidate Kremlin policy during the Second World War. An interpretation of this policy is almost thrust upon us if we analyse the strategic situation of the summer of 1940 from Moscow's viewpoint, and consider this analysis in the light of the authoritative Soviet military doctrine of the time – the dogma of the class-conditioned inferiority of the 'capitalist' and 'imperialist' armies and the consequent belief in an 'easy victory'.

Up to this point, the Moor had rendered excellent service: he had made possible, without trouble or risk for the Soviet Union, the annexation of the eastern Polish regions, remained loyal in the Finnish War and – a factor of particular importance – prevented the Allies from establishing a flanking position in the north. In the west he had proved his worth in brilliant fashion, though in an unexpected way – the long-drawn-out war of attrition had not come to pass and nowhere had there been any trace of a revolutionary situation. Without knowing it or wanting to, the Germans had performed a surprising and very important service for Moscow: they had eliminated the military capacity of Russia's most important opponents, the Western powers, from the continent. France's divisions had been crushed, the British driven back across the Channel; and even with possible future help from the U.S.A. they would be unable to mount an assault on the continent for years to come.

This sequence of events brought about a completely new strategical situation, the significance of which, oddly enough, has hitherto scarcely been noticed, let alone given due weight. The Western 'imperialists' had lost their position of power on the continent, and only the Wehrmacht stood between the Red Army and the Atlantic. If the German army was defeated, the Soviets would be masters of the European continent and so, potentially at least, of the whole of the Ancient World; and Britain and America would be powerless to prevent them.

The Kremlin could now hardly expect to make any more use of Germany. Having reaching the Atlantic coast, the German army was at the limit of its capabilities and could not win any more significant successes against the Western powers. An invasion across the Channel would have been an absurdly risky venture, while there was no practical possibility of an attack on America, for the British and American navies were far superior in the Atlantic. Besides, any further increase in Germany's power was not in Moscow's interests, and Stalin was beginning to wonder what new task the German dictator would set his land forces, most of which were now available for other duties. It was, indeed, quite probable that he would now turn his attention to areas where German and Russian interests vied with each other. As a result of the situation created by the campaign in France, the man who had so far been a help was now developing into a hindrance, whose removal – within the framework of the magical doctrine of the 'easy victory' – wouldn't seem to be too great a task.

There are many clues to suggest that Stalin quickly came to grips with the new situation and soon resolved to make the most of this unique opportunity which had fallen into his lap as a result of the Western campaign. The details of the process by which he came to his conclusion will always remain a subject of conjecture, but in any case the decision lay between two possibilities. The first was to continue with the present policy – keep out of the war and engage in massive rearmament, initially seeking strictly limited successes and only making a decisive appearance on the scene when the antagonists had exhausted themselves. For various reasons this patient and watchful approach might appear advisable, but the Soviet leader had to appreciate that time wasn't working for him alone. Once the enormous war potential of the U.S.A. had swung into action and British and American forces had opened one or more fronts on the continent, then these two stronger opponents would soon occupy a position of power in Europe and hegemony would have to be shared with them. The other possibility was to use this opportunity to defeat the German army in a victorious campaign and thus present the rest of the world with a *fait accompli*. The prerequisite of such an action was, of course, that no agreement should be reached between Germany and Great Britain or the U.S.A.

During the campaign in the west it had become obvious that England under Churchill had no intention of coming to an understanding with Germany, and the sinking of the French Fleet at Oran by the British on 3 July 1940 gave ample evidence of their bellicose intentions. This fulfilled the most important precondition for a new Soviet policy and strategy, which was now aimed with renewed vigour directly against Germany, but indirectly against the 'imperialists' of the West – as far as possible without them knowing it.

The existence of this two-pronged strategy – which allowed Germany, as before, to be used as a tool against the Western powers – can be proved by documentary evidence. For example, a telegram sent by the Soviet Foreign Office, dated 8 March 1941 and intercepted by German intelligence, ran as follows:

> The Soviet Union will not interfere with the German action against Greece: this is needed to exert pressure on the English colonies, to threaten the Suez Canal, to hold up supplies for English troops in Africa. On the other hand the mood of the Balkan Countries is increasingly against involvement in the war. We must warn the Balkan governments supporting Germany that this may endanger peace in the Balkans; we must exert pressure on Yugoslavia and Turkey, so that they don't support any one side in the war, and at the same time solicit the goodwill of the Greek people, who must fight the German invasion. While pointing out what we have stated above, we must at the same time also emphasise that we have no intention of endangering the German-Russian treaty, which is necessary to fulfil our most urgent aim, namely, the destruction of the British Empire.

The thinking of the Soviet leaders at this time is also revealed by a statement made by Molotov on 30 June 1940 to the Lithuanian Foreign Minister Kreve-Mickevicius:

> We are now more than ever convinced that our brilliant comrade Lenin made no mistake when he asserted that the Second World War would enable us to seize power in Europe, just as we did in Russia after the First World War. For this reason you should be starting now to introduce your people into the Soviet system, which in future will rule all Europe.[100]

In this way Hitler was to be used as a battering ram against the allegedly strongest bastion of capitalism, Great Britain, but at the same time the Soviet leaders wanted to preserve the semblance of loyalty to the Germans, perhaps with the idea of thrusting onto them, at the coming clash of arms, the role of treaty-breaking aggressor. Furthermore, in the summer of 1944 the Soviets allowed German troops to put down the revolt of the national Polish secret army in Warsaw; and, indeed, the German dictator did his Soviet counterpart a final good turn in December 1944 when he used up his last battle-worthy units in the Ardennes offensive against the Allies, and so exposed eastern Germany to the Red Army.

It cannot be stated exactly when the decision was made to embark on this strategy, but the essay from *The Red Dawn* quoted at the beginning of this chapter indicates that it was adopted as soon as it was realised that the campaign in the west was a great success, and the actual behaviour of the Soviets around this time tends to support this idea. The first phase of Soviet expansion had kept within the framework of the agreement between Hitler and Stalin. This applied to the annexation of eastern Poland and the establishment of Russian bases in the Baltic states, but also to the Winter War against Finland, in which Hitler maintained his loyalty towards his partner even though this led to a worsening of relations with the Finns. However, when it became obvious that the British would be expelled from the continent and that the French would collapse, the Baltic states and Rumania were subjected to Russian pressure – which increased noticeably even though Berlin let it be known that a forcible occupation of Bessarabia at this time would be regarded by Germany and Italy as an unfriendly act.[101]

All this indicates that the Kremlin was now inclined to ignore the wishes of its partner. In mid-June 1940 the Soviets moved strong forces first into Lithuania, then into Latvia and Estonia, and began a comprehensive Sovietisation of these areas. (There were, however, no mass deportations till the spring of 1941). At the end of the month Rumania had to submit to a Russian ultimatum, which Germany was unable to prevent, and at the same time Moscow signified its interest in the Balkans by taking up diplomatic relations with Yugoslavia. The annexation of the Baltic states and Bessarabia could be justified by stating that the Soviets only wanted to assure the safety of the former Russian regions allocated to them by the Hitler–Stalin Pact, but in two places they had already violated the agreed borders defining the spheres of interest. In the south-west of Lithuania they had occupied a strip of land around the town of Mariampol, allocated to Germany under the pact, and in Rumania they took over northern Bukovina with Czernovitz, which had never belonged to the czarist empire. Some German circles saw this as a move by the Kremlin to take quick possession of its booty in advance of a potential German peace treaty with England. This turned out to be nothing but wishful thinking. Molotov's visit to Berlin in November 1940 soon revealed the political and strategic intentions currently motivating Soviet activities.

In the last days of June 1940 pressure was also increased on Finland,[102] which the pact included in the Russian sphere of interest, but in the Winter War the Russians had first to agree to a compromise peace in order to avoid a collision with the Western powers. With their defeat, this danger was removed, so the Kremlin could set about forcing the fulfilment of this further agreement in the Hitler–Stalin Pact, an action which opened up a serious conflict between the partners in the 1939 treaty. In view of the British unwillingness to compromise, it was becoming increasingly clear to the German leaders that they would have to fight a long war with uncertain prospects; they were also being made aware of the folly they had committed by handing over Finland to an opponent whose attitude was becoming more and more devious, since this country was important not only for its minerals, especially the nickel of Petsamo, but also because its position on the flank gave it strategic and military importance. Berlin therefore decided to support the Finns – at first discreetly, later more openly. So began a game of move and counter-move between the two opponents, the details of which we can pass over at this stage. A similar, but more important game began in the Balkan and Danube regions – which, because of their agrarian products, ores and especially the Rumanian oilfields, were of vital economic interest, while their position on the flank also gave them strategic importance. This position will be discussed later.

In the meantime the Soviet rearmament went ahead with increased vigour. On 26 June 1940, the day after the ratification of the armistice with France, the top presidency of the Supreme Soviet of the U.S.S.R. issued a decree '. . . concerning the transition to the eight-hour working day and the seven-day week and the prohibition of unauthorized absence from works and offices by workers'; another decree tightened up work discipline among tractor and combine-harvester drivers and allied trades. These measures were intended to fortify the military strength of the country,[103] but it would appear that they were not very successful at first; nor was it very clear what motives and intentions were behind this renewed increase in the speed of rearmament, which had already been accelerated since 1939.

Soon, however, the new course became more apparent. Moscow received the British recommendations brought over by Sir Stafford Cripps with cautious restraint, and criticised especially the suggestions for a re-establishment of the balance of power in Europe – in other words, the arrangement created after the First World War. After all, the Soviet Union had achieved its position in eastern and central Europe by destroying this very arrangement. Cripps also gave to understand that London was prepared to make greater concessions than Berlin in the Balkans, a fact which the Kremlin certainly took careful notice of but did not set too much store by. Stalin told the British Ambassador that he wanted to avoid an open conflict with Germany for the present, but was expecting to face a German attack in the spring of 1941, provided that England had been conquered by then. At about the same time Yugoslav Ambassador Gavrilovic got the impression in conversation that the Soviet Union had no fear of Germany and was quickly making preparations to meet an invasion, but wished to swing Yugoslavia against the Germans. For the time being, at least, the Kremlin wanted to avoid a war with Germany, preferring to pursue its interests indirectly. The report on this subject which Gavrilovic sent to Belgrade soon became known to the Foreign Office in Berlin.[104]

During these conversations Molotov spoke very deprecatingly about the Germans, saying that they were no better than the Italians.[105] Bearing this in mind, the speech which the Foreign Minister delivered on 1 August 1940 to the Supreme Soviet is of especial interest. He made a slight threat against Finland and a more definite one against Turkey, thus giving some idea of the next Soviet ambitions. However, both moves would conflict with German interests. The last sentences of the speech are more revealing:

In these circumstances the Soviet Union must be on her guard, especially with respect to her safety from foreign intrusion . . . We have started the eight-hour day in place of the previous seven-hour day and are taking other measures, for we consider it our duty to develop and secure our capacity to defend ourselves . . . We have had many successes, but we don't intend to be satisfied with what we have achieved. In order to guarantee further essential successes, we must always keep Stalin's words in our minds. We must keep our whole nation in a state of mobilisation, of preparedness for a military attack, so that no 'accident' and no tricks on the part of our foreign enemies can find us unprepared. If we all continue to bear this in mind, this our sacred duty, then nothing that happens could surprise us, and we will gain even more glorious successes for the Soviet Union. [106]

These statements raise a number of questions and suggest definite answers. Who was to lead this military attack? Certainly not Great Britain, which was incapable of such a venture in the aftermath of its recent defeat and was openly paying court to Moscow. Where and against whom were these even more glorious victories for the Soviet Union to be gained? This could hardly apply to Britain, and certainly not to Finland or Turkey alone. Only Germany could be considered as a possible aggressor, and thus Germany could also be the victim of the glorious victories. It is not impossible that even at this stage Moscow had much information about the deliberations of Hitler and the German High Command concerning the possibility of a campaign in the east in July. However, the way the repulse of an attack and the winning of glorious victories are named in one and the same breath admits of a quite different interpretation, especially when considered together with the doctrine of an 'easy victory' and the 'crushing of the aggressor on his territory'. Is there not here some trace of a desire to provoke Germany into making an attack in order then to inflict a defeat by counter-attack, and so gain mastery over the continent of Europe?

The Foreign Minister naturally avoided openly formulating such intentions in a speech intended for the public. He restricted himself to hints, accompanied by protestations of loyalty towards Germany and attacks on the Anglo-American 'imperialists' and 'warmongers'.

The influence of Soviet military doctrine of the time on political and strategic decision-making in the Kremlin has hitherto not been considered very much, although it is indispensable if one is to understand Stalin's actions. This may be due to the fact that the doctrine was dramatically refuted by the heavy defeat of the Red Army in the summer and autumn of 1941, and because in many quarters it was held to be nothing more than the expression of an excess of self-esteem based on ideological illusions. In this case, however, it is not a question of the correctness or falseness of the doctrine, but of the precedence it had in the thought processes and resolutions of the Soviet leaders at the time.

The dogma, spread by propaganda and usually also believed, of the superiority in principle of the socialist over the capitalist system, was not without influence in military circles. Encouragement in this belief was given by Engels, who had stated that the members of a socialist society,

... in the case of a war, which in any case would only be against anti-communist nations, had a real fatherland, a real home to defend, so that they would fight with such enthusiasm, endurance and bravery that the soldiers of a modern army, drilled to mechanical obedience, would scatter before them like chaff in the wind.[107]

Such convictions were cherished a long time before the Second World War:

Soviet military science is in accordance with the possibilities inherent in the structure of the Soviet state and society; it reflects the incomparable superiority of the Soviet armed forces over the armies of the capitalist countries, and in the hands of the Soviet people will prove to be a powerful weapon for victorious warfare against the enemies of the socialist state.[108]

The military doctrine of the Red Army was also founded on this basic conviction in the years before the outbreak of war. In the regulations and instructions, as well as in the ideas behind operational and strategical wargames, the thought of the victorious *attack* was always expressed as the active method of warfare – as was stated, for example, in the plans for the field service regiments in the year 1939:

The Union of the Soviet Socialist Republics will answer every attack with a destructive blow from the whole might of their armed forces. Our war against the attacker will be the most just war in the history of mankind. If the enemy forces war on us, then the Red Army will be the most offensive of all armies. We will wage an offensive war and carry it right into the territory of our opponents. The fighting methods of the Red Army will be annihilating . . .[109]

The Soviet Union felt itself more and more in the position,

. . . in the case of war, to set itself decisive, strategic goals, which went as far as *completely wiping out the enemy aggressor on his own territory*.[110]

As must be emphasised again, this was not merely propaganda and rhetoric, but the basis upon which the armed forces were founded and the guiding principle in the training of its staff and troops. A massive engagement of tank units, co-operating with motorised infantry and air forces and supported by heavy artillery, would signal the beginning of an attack and perform the task of breaking up enemy formations by annihilating blows throughout their full depth. The grouping for attack demanded an echelon formation, whose first assault was designed to achieve a breakthrough into the enemy positions, while the second, using mobile forces, was to press forward into the gaps, overtake the retreating enemy, and destroy or encircle him together with his reserves.[111] These tactics were confirmed by observation of the motorised war as exemplified by the German army in Poland and France.

Stalin regarded this doctrine as his 'new theory', and he ordered it to be tried out in wargames and exercises during the winter of 1940–41.[112] Questions arising from the theory were discussed in very great detail at a conference in Moscow at the end of December 1940, attended by leading military advisers, amongst them Timoschenko and Schukov. There were discussions of attack operations by mechanised and tank units; the creation of tank corps or armies after the German model was demanded; and the problem of massing mobile forces was examined. In conclusion, the People's Commissar for Defence emphasised the significance of high-speed attack, which made an irresistible breakthrough in depth possible – provided it was carried out by the concentrated advance of mechanised ground troops, backed by air force units. After this conference a high-level wargame led by Marshal Timoschenko took place, at which the principles for large-scale strategic operations were tried out and the potential theatres of war discussed. Marshal Yeremenko summarised the results as follows: 'We had sufficient forces not only to halt the enemy offensive but also to deal him a crushing defeat by means of counter-strikes and a counter-offensive.'[113] Stalin's faulty planning, he asserted, was to blame for the debacle of the summer of 1941. General Kirponos, Supreme Commander of the South-west Army Group, made similar remarks just before the commencement of hostilities: 'Most probably we will form a strong attack unit and make a determined counter-offensive against the enemy.' Later Marshal Vassilevski gave more details:

> Our infantry brigades had the task, together with the border defence troops and the strong points of the military border regions, of holding up the first attack. The mechanised corps, exploiting the anti-tank lines together with the infantry, had the task of liquidating the groups which had broken into our defences and creating favourable conditions for our own attacks. By the beginning of the enemy's attack, forces coming up from inside the U.S.S.R. should have reached the military border regions. It was also assumed that in any case our troops would be fully prepared and could join the war in organised groupings, after completing their mobilisation.

But the German attack took place too soon:

> However, we did not succeed in completing the mobilisation and gen-

eral organisation as planned. This was partly owing to an erroneous forecast as to the time of a possible fascist attack on our country, but it must also be stated that the economic limitations of the country made it impossible to carry out all the measures needed in the time left to us.[114]

In accordance with Stalin's 'new theory', the tactical training of staffs and troops was, and would remain, one-sidedly directed towards attack. Defence and retreat were to a large extent neglected, as the Soviet Union discovered to its cost when the war started. Marshal Bagramian wrote later:

> Before the war we had learned . . . mostly to attack. We had not paid enough attention to such an important matter as a retreat. Now we had to pay for that failing.[115]

The same applied to the strategic and operational level. The Soviet deployment in the spring of 1941 depended – as will be explained later in more detail (page 104) – on the assumption that a German attack could be repulsed by an immediate counter-attack, which would be the start of a large-scale offensive. This was the reason for the concentration of the Red Army in the vicinity of the border, a fact which fell in with the German plan of attack and made an essential contribution to the initial successes achieved.[116]

Another contributory factor to the belief in an 'easy victory' over the fascist aggressors was the illusion that, as it advanced, the Red Army would be enthusiastically greeted and actively supported by the oppressed workers; it was even believed that a revolution could break out behind the enemy lines and hasten the triumph of the Soviet liberators. This idea also played an important role in Soviet propaganda. For example, the following statement was made about the occupation of eastern Poland:

> On 17 September the freedom army of workers and peasants, the army of the Soviet Union – which consists of many states and whose flags bear the noble words: Brotherhood of Nations, Socialism and Peace – began the most just campaign ever known to humanity. This army of liberation will be greeted as no liberation army has ever been greeted . . . It comes, this army of liberation, this army of the Soviet Union, this great friend of all suppressed peoples, it comes with the name of Stalin on its lips; it awakens hope, joy in life and confidence . . .[117]

A tendency to trivialise German successes to date was also evident: the Polish army had been lacking in modern equipment and national unity;[118] the defeat of the French had been due to the activity of a fifth column supporting Hitler and the fact that the appeasement policy of the western bourgeoisie had divided those forces which could have beaten off the fascist aggression.

> The fateful effects of these actions was made even worse by the persecution of progressive forces at the start of the war – especially the communists in France, England and other countries.

Such is the opinion of *Die Geschichte*.[119] It was either unaware of or preferred to ignore the fact that the communists left no stone unturned – using propaganda, subversion and sabotage – in their efforts to thwart the French war effort (see pages 55 ff).

Besides, the opinion, widely held in pre-war Russia, that victory over the enemy would be easily gained[120] had many detrimental consequences, as was later freely admitted by Marshal Vassilevski, Chief of the Soviet General Staff from 1942 to 1944:

> It must be stated here that the basically correct guideline which indicates that in the case of an attack on the Soviet Union the Soviet troops should be made to act resolutely and carry the war into the territory of the enemy has in many places become a dogma which nourishes the illusion of an easy victory . . . [121]

Even if this feeling of superiority turned out to be illusory, it was by no means completely unjustified and did to some extent derive from the actual strength of the Red Army and the efficiency of the armaments industry. The real potential of both these was proved in the war when the Russians showed themselves capable of recovering with extraordinary speed from the heavy losses of the first months and then thrusting at the enemy ever-increasing masses of men and material. These achievements are all the more astonishing because at the time important industrial and raw-materials-producing areas had been lost and could not be replaced by the transfer of numerous armaments factories up to and beyond the Urals. The supply lines from the Western powers were at this stage still in their infancy and would only play an important role later on.[122] This proves unambiguously how great Soviet superiority would have been, were it not for the unforeseen reverses of the first war years.

Numerically, this superiority can only be defined approximately, but in many areas it was quite distinct, as is shown by a comparison of the strength of the attacker with the Russian losses in the first year of the war. At the beginning of the campaign, the German army had in the east a total of more than 3,050,000 men, 7,184 pieces of artillery, 3,580 tanks and 2,740 aircraft.[123] On the other side, according to German figures relating only to the encirclement actions of Bialystok–Minsk and Smolensk till the middle of July, no less than 642,000 prisoners were brought in, while 4,929 pieces of artillery and 6,537 tanks were captured or destroyed.[124] If these figures are prone to inaccuracy or exaggeration, they nevertheless appear credible in view of evidence from Soviet sources, since the Soviet Information Office gives the following figures for losses in the first year of the war: 4,500,000 men killed, wounded or taken prisoner, 22,000 heavy guns, 15,000 tanks and 9,000 aircraft.[125] This is also the verdict of the British military expert John Erickson: 'If one applies Stalin's figures, based on Soviet sources, Soviet superiority amounted to seven to one in tanks, at least; in aircraft the Germans were inferior in the ratio of four or five to one.'[126]

Even though a large number of the aircraft and tanks were out of date, there were also a considerable number of new types available at the outbreak of war. In the first six months of 1941 alone 2,653 bomber and fighter aircraft were built to modern designs; by the middle of June the army had received 1,861 tanks of the KW and T34 types.[127] The legendary T34 was definitely superior to its German equivalent and almost invulnerable to the current anti-tank weapons of its opponents. From January 1939 to 22 June 1941 more than 7,000 armoured vehicles were delivered, and in the year 1941 about 5,500 tanks of all types were delivered.[128] To equip the motorised units – those in the planning stage as well as those already operational – 16,600 of the new tanks were available, with about 32,000 projected – an enormous number. It seems most improbable that this avalanche of tanks was only intended for defence purposes.[129] The only type of German tank in any way comparable with the new Soviet designs was the Panzer IV, but of these only 618 were operational at the beginning of the Eastern campaign; otherwise motorised units were equipped mainly with Kampfwagen II and III (armoured cars).[130]

At the beginning of 1941 monthly production amounted to only 250 tanks and heavy field guns.[131]

Soviet superiority in artillery was the most marked. Archive documents reveal that from 1 January 1939 to 22 June 1941 the Red Army received a total of 29,637 field guns and 52,407 trench mortars, making, together with the tank guns, a total 92,578 big guns and mortars.[132] Of these the rocket launchers ('Stalin's Organs') were a particularly unpleasant surprise for the attacker.[133]

These and other figures show clearly enough that the Soviet belief in the military and industrial strength of the Fatherland was far more than a mere *fata morgana*. The Soviet Union of this period already contained the nucleus of a future superpower. Why, in spite of this, it suffered the heavy defeats of the first phase of the war will be discussed later (pages 112 ff).

The main question, however, is not how far this feeling of superiority was justified, but how crucial a part it played in Soviet policy decisions during the period before the German invasion. The facts dealt with so far, and also the likely deployment of Soviet forces in the spring of 1941 (see pages 104 ff), would in any case seem to indicate that Soviet leaders were counting on their ability to repulse an attack immediately, then go on to destroy the aggressor on his own territory and so be able to celebrate the 'easy victory'.

Germany: Despair and Audacity

In Germany the idea of a military clash with the Soviet Union was steadily taking root. In view of the lack of documentary evidence, no comment can be made as to whether Moscow had any knowledge of this. All thoughts and reflections on this point[134] were at first restricted to Hitler and his close associates, and for some time there were no troop movements or changes affecting the country's economy or arms production which might have hinted at aggressive intentions towards the Soviet Union.

The events leading up to Operation Barbarossa have been frequently described, using the mass of available documentary evidence, so that at this juncture a very brief sketch should suffice. The whole episode clearly shows that Hitler was an amateur, certainly not without talent, but quite incapable of logical planning on a large scale and entirely lacking in the statesmanlike qualities of astuteness or foresight in the field of world politics. One can follow his ragged train of thought – how he seized on certain ideas, busied himself with them for a while, put them away, brought them out again, until eventually he found himself in an embarrassing situation from which he imagined he could only escape by violent means.

Having said that, it should be acknowledged that the attack on the Soviet Union was impelled by two ideas which thread their way through the Führer's 'philosophy of life'. One was the idea of obtaining by conquest *Lebensraum* in the east for the German people – a concept which had already been discussed in connection with the occupation of the Ukraine in 1918. There, the German empire was to gain a region for settlement – which he considered to be a good starting point for any future aspirations to world power, both from the point of view of population policy and also for military and economic reasons. The other guiding principle – if such it can be called – of Hitler's life was concerned with the ideology of race, or, to put it more precisely, the subjection and enslavement of the 'subhuman' Slav and the annihilation of

'Jewish Bolshevism'. For tactical reasons both these motives were sometimes pushed into the background for a while, and at times they were neglected for other considerations, but they were always present just below the surface.

These ideas should be distinguished from those trains of thought which resulted from the practical exigencies of the war, and therefore changed as the conflict developed – from the euphoria after the victory in the west to the attempt, in a mixture of audacity and despair,[135] to break through the 'iron ring' which eventually began to close around Germany. Whether the two ideas mentioned or the concrete political and strategic aspects played the more important role in the various phases of Hitler's decision-making is open to question. At any rate, from the date of Molotov's visit to Berlin in November 1940, the Führer found himself in the position of a gambler who has to play his last card.

It is well known that, shortly after the armistice with France, Hitler stated that he only needed to provide a demonstration of military might to make Britain seek peace, thus leaving the bulk of German forces free for a campaign in the east.[136] He certainly had in mind the mistrust which the Soviets had aroused by their advances during his campaign in France. However, when Britain persisted in her unyielding attitude he also suspected that, with France effectively out of the equation, the British were hoping to persuade the Soviet Union to oppose Hitler on the mainland of Europe, which did indeed happen. On top of this, fears about the U.S.A. were assuming ever more alarming proportions. The German General Staff therefore began to give serious thought to preparations for a campaign in the east – which at this time was not aimed at the total subjection of the Soviet Union, but had the primary intention of driving Soviet forces so far back that they couldn't bomb Berlin or the Silesian industrial regions, while the Luftwaffe would be in a position to devastate the most important areas of the Soviet Union. From the point of view of territorial gains, at least, these goals were far more modest than the extreme German plans for the east during the First World War.[137]

The military and political outlook for Germany began to look more and more gloomy. Britain remained obdurate and Hitler was forced to realise that he had not the means at his disposal to conquer the British Isles by direct attack. Operation Sea Lion, the plan for a cross-Channel invasion, was so fraught with hazards that finally the Führer fought shy of it. The Germany navy, especially after the losses suffered in the wake of the invasion of Norway, was far inferior to the British, and control of the skies over the Channel remained unattainable – indeed, Germany's pilots suffered their first heavy defeat over England. Even more serious consequences resulted from Italy's entry into the war. Its economic dependence on Germany soon became a serious handicap, and the defeats inflicted on the Italians by the British had not only strategic but also psychological and political significance. The Axis powers were beginning to wear a vulnerable look.

Thus a situation was developing which Hitler could not cope with and which he sought to master with insufficient means. The preparations for Operation Sea Lion were carried on halfheartedly, and at the same time consideration was given to plans to exert pressure on the British at the periphery, by weakening their Mediterranean position through the occupation of Gibraltar. For various reasons, however, these plans could not be carried out.

The failure of the political sphere was even more evident. The German dictator was looking for allies:

> If England insists on continuing the war, then we will try to use other countries politically against England: Spain, Italy, Russia.[138]

But that was easier said than done. The Führer failed in his attempt to bring the very different interests of Spain, Italy and France under one common denominator – a task which would have daunted a far more capable politician. In the meantime America under President Roosevelt was increasing its support for the hard-pressed British and an open declaration of war moved threateningly nearer; and the tension with the Soviet Union became more and more acute, especially in the Balkan and Danube regions. The conclusion of the Three Power Pact with Italy and Japan on 27 September 1940 was little more than a formal confirmation of the existing situation. The hope of using this alliance to put America under pressure soon turned out to be an illusion. This pact provided for the possibility of inducing the Soviets to join and so creating a continental bloc of the four powers, which was intended to make the British and Americans think twice before invading the Eurasian continent or Africa.

It is possible that Hitler did not believe that this project had much prospect of success, so in these tension-laden months he pursued a kind of twin strategy against Moscow. Although he was preparing for a clash of arms, he didn't want to slam the door in the face of a political solution – or even an interim solution. But during the late summer and autumn German–Soviet relations developed in such a manner that a solution of this kind looked more and more improbable. Moscow increased the pressure on western areas and sought especially to use the tensions between Bulgaria, Rumania and Hungary for its own purposes. This caused Hitler to block any further Soviet penetration in this direction by means of the Second Vienna Verdict and the guarantee of the

Rumanian border on 30 August 1940 – a move which evoked considerable ill-feeling in Moscow. Ribbentrop's amateurish and careless behaviour in his former dealings with Stalin were being dearly paid for. After the annexation of Bessarabia, the Russians could declare that they had never – verbally or in writing – recognised that Germany was the 'only power with an exclusive interest in Rumania'.[139] Cautiously but unshakably, they pursued their plans for the Balkans, trying at first to get the Danube delta under their control. In a surprise action at the end of October 1940 the Red Army occupied some Rumanian islands in the main arm of the delta, thus not only gaining strategic advantages, but also intentionally defying the German guarantee. Moscow was also seeking a political settlement on its own terms. It demanded the dissolution of the European Danube Commission, created in 1856 after the Crimean War, which exercised rights of sovereignty in the Lower Danube basin. This authority, in which England and France had a seat and a vote, had been set up as a barrier against Soviet ambitions to the south towards the Straits or along the open Danube waterway and right into the heart of Europe.[140] Moscow wanted this authority to be replaced, at least provisionally, by a Soviet–Rumanian administration of the Lower Danube – including all the arms of the delta – in which the Soviets would naturally have an overwhelming majority and by which they would be able to exercise a dominant influence on the whole of the Danube area. It was also intended that passage through the Sulina arm of the river should be granted to merchant ships of all nations, but only to Soviet and Rumanian warships.[141] These proposals are also significant because in Berlin Molotov expressed interest in a similar regulation of the exit passages from the Baltic.

The Kremlin's diplomatic game with the British and the Axis powers is particularly interesting. When Sir Stafford Cripps protested in Moscow about the suppression of the European Danube Commission and declared that his government would not give up its rights, he was given an answer in a note, which was also published. It stated that the Soviet Union was under no obligation to take any notice of Britain, which had excluded the Soviet Union from all commissions at Versailles dealing with the Danube. Moreover, it was a long way from Britain and was none of her business.[142] Thus it was made clear to the British, in an absolutely offensive manner, who – according to the Soviet viewpoint – was lord of the manor on the Lower Danube. By doing this the Kremlin sought to announce publicly its loyalty to the Axis powers (and especially Germany), while at the same time trying to drive them from the Lower Danube in order to gain complete control of the area from Galatz to Sulina.

In October 1940, at the request of Bucharest, the Germans had sent a military commission to Rumania which was followed in November by a 'training force' with the strength of about one division, and a few air force units; in December a tank division was also sent. This despatch of forces might have been considered completely legitimate, since according to the Berlin interpretation of the 1939 treaties Rumania now belonged entirely to the German sphere of interest and had requested the despatch of these troops, but this move was also deemed necessary in order to emphasis, by at least a symbolic military presence, the guarantee given to the land. These units would have been much too weak for any large-scale operations, and in Finland, which by the Moscow agreements had been handed over to the Soviet sphere of interest, the Germans were even more cautious. Yet in both cases Hitler wanted to indicate that he had no intention of giving in to Soviet pressure. This was also understood in the Kremlin.

During these months Hitler the politician generally gave the impression of a man who feels that his control of the situation is slipping away from him and so is looking for a way out, but finds that one alternative after another proves to be impossible. This is reflected in the mood prevailing in Germany at the time. The euphoria and anticipation of peace hopes which had characterised the early summer gave way to an atmosphere of uncertainty, even worry. Although many still believed in the 'divine Führer', the Adolf Hitler beloved of Providence and Fate, others were noting with sorrow how the hostile world coalition foreseen by General Beck was marshalling its forces.

The dictator still thought he had a trump card to play with – the German Army. But his uncertainty concerning the future also influenced his military dispositions, as well as those concerning the country's economy and arms production. The operational studies of the General Staff during this time, the actual troop movements, and the instructions to the armament industry – all are more expressive of helplessness than of far-seeing and methodical planning: the planned landing in England was postponed from one date to the next and finally put off till 1941; the Italians needed urgent support after suffering heavy defeats; a conquest of Gibraltar was planned; consideration was given to obtaining bases in French North Africa and the Cape Verde Islands, as well as sending an expedition to the Suez Canal. In all this, England was still regarded as the main enemy. Only after the Molotov visit did the Soviet Union take centre stage.

The actual distribution of troops also fits in with this picture. Directly after the victory in France it was planned to demobilise a large number of divisions or send them home on leave. This was partly carried out, which suggests that no large-scale military operation was planned. The transfer of the Eighteenth Army to Prussia and Poland, which followed in the course of July, was nothing more than a safety measure – the east had been left almost completely exposed during the campaign in the west. The forces gathered together in Army Group B didn't reach the strength of thirty-five divisions in this eastern area until the end of October: of these, six were tank divisions and one a cavalry division. Army Groups A and D remained for the time being in the west, while Group C remained in Germany.

> Nothing characterises better the irresoluteness of the German leadership regarding the continuance of military operations than the approximately equal distribution of German forces in Hitler-dominated territory prior to the crucial discussions with Molotov. There was a little more emphasis on the west, but not much.[143]

This lack of clarity in the direction of the war economy and the arms industry was especially evident where long-term planning was most necessary. Instead, Hitler ordered repeated changes, all of short duration; degrees of urgency were fixed, and soon altered again; orders were made, and then countermanded by other orders. In the confusion, which would not have escaped the notice of Soviet intelligence, there is very little evidence of a definite decision on Hitler's part to attack the Soviet Union in the spring of 1941. The department of the military dealing with armaments and the economy was just as much groping in the dark about the further course of the war as the High Command and General Staff, not to mention Hitler himself.[144]

But the theoretical preparations for the campaign in the east were not abandoned. As has already been mentioned, Hitler had considered such a campaign soon after the victory in France. He had even thought of starting the attack in August 1940, but that had been found impossible for military and technical reasons[145] – troop deployments would have taken up to four months. The start of this possible operation had therefore to be put off until the spring of 1941. Originally the dictator had hoped to get Britain to surrender and free him for the attack on the Soviet Union, but during the course of the summer he had to admit that such a development was no longer feasible. The unbroken will to fight of the British and the possible entry into the war of the U.S.A. now had to be included in his calculations, and it amounted to the threat of an armed clash with a power bloc whose war potential was vastly superior to that of Germany. Thus Hitler's dependence on Russia, which he had stumbled into by his pact with Stalin, had been considerably increased. In those fateful months the attitude of Moscow was, to put it mildly, ambiguous and incalculable, so the Führer had to bear in mind that they could exploit this embarrassing situation at any time.

The danger of a war on two fronts, the avoidance of which had always been one of the dictator's main aims, was now increasingly real. One

81

possible escape route was a political solution, by which the Soviets were to be tied up in a three-nation pact, diverted in the south towards the Persian Gulf and India, and thus hopefully involved in a conflict with England. However, even if they fell in with this plan everything still depended on their loyalty, and Hitler had every reason to mistrust Stalin, just as the latter mistrusted Hitler. The alternative was to fight it out on the field of battle. If, in view of the threatening confrontation with the West, the Führer was not happy to be solely dependent on the goodwill of Moscow, then he was compelled to try to defeat the Soviet Union by force of arms, and so obtain by conquest an extraterritorial sphere of influence in the east which would be unaffected by the blockade. To the previous motives of the need for *Lebensraum* and the 'struggle against Jewish Bolshevism' was now added Hitler's current embarrassing situation, which he could only remedy by a decisive victory over the Soviet Union before Britain and the U.S.A. could bring their full war potential to bear on Germany. Hitler wanted to keep this option open regardless of the outcome of the negotiations with Moscow. This is clear from his 'Instruction No. 18' of 12 November 1940:

> Political discussions have been initiated with the object of clarifying Russia's attitude for the near future. Irrespective of the results yielded by these discussions, all orally ordered preparations for the east are to be continued.

Basically, both opponents were fighting for time. They had to act before the might of the British and Americans could intervene actively on the continent – the Soviets would have to act if they wanted to conquer the continent of Europe, the Germans if they wanted to avoid a war on two fronts and gain a blockade-free extra-territorial sphere of interest.

The whole situation of the Axis powers had considerably deteriorated since the end of the campaign in the west, but Hitler suffered a series of further reverses shortly before the Russian Foreign Minister arrived in Berlin. The discussions whch he had with France in Hendaye on 23 October, and the next day with Pétain in Montoire, yielded no results – obviously these two experienced army commanders did not take a very optimistic view of Germany's military situation. On 20 October Mussolini's foolish attack on Greece, the result of injured vanity, created a dangerous focal point for crisis in the Balkans. On 5 November the re-election of Roosevelt brought the entry of the U.S.A. into the war still nearer, and just before Molotov's arrival in Berlin the Italian offensive was halted in the mountains on the Greek border. In view of all these circumstances, the guest from Moscow felt himself to be in a position of strength.

Extortion and Provocation

It is the generally-held opinion among non-Soviet historians that Molotov's discussions with Hitler and Ribbentrop were one of the most important political events of the Second World War, and made a decisive contribution to the later clash between Germany and the Soviet Union. It is all the more striking that Soviet accounts of the meeting glide over it in a few short passages. For example, the semi-official (and monumental) *Geschichte* limits its account to these few words:

> In November 1940 negotiations took place between the U.S.S.R. and Germany. The government of the U.S.S.R. made every effort to protect Bulgaria from the threatened German occupation. The German leaders thereupon suggested that borders be drawn up to define their mutual spheres of interest. This was obviously an endeavour to bring Soviet foreign policy under German control. The Soviet Union should recognise German and Italian sovereignty in Europe and Africa and Japanese sovereignty in Asia, but in its own international policy should limit itself exclusively to the area south of the Soviet state in the direction of the Indian Ocean. In return for this, the German government would recognise the territorial inviolability of the Soviet Union. The Soviet Union preserved her national independence and sovereignty. It was opposed to the imperialist policy of creating spheres of influence and rejected the German proposals.[146]

The fact that in the previous year Stalin and Hitler had implemented a similar 'imperialist policy' is no more mentioned here than are the demands which Stalin's ambassador handed over to his German counterparts at the discussions; nor is there any revelation at all of other Soviet intentions, which went far beyond these demands. Telpuchovski does not mention the Molotov visit at all, Besymenski devotes a few meaningless words to it,[147] and even the memoirs of Valentin Bereshkov, interpreter and secretary to the embassy at the time, skilfully avoid the awkward points.[148] In fact, Hillgruber mentions a Soviet special assignment,

. . . for their own secret police and also for the 'Ulbricht Group', just after the Red Army entered Berlin in May 1945, ordering them to put into safe-keeping all recordings of the Hitler–Ribbentrop–Molotov discussions found in the archives of the Hauses des Rundfunks.[149]

All this makes it seem probable that happenings of extraordinary importance have – on the Soviet side – been covered up.

It is therefore fitting that this historical event should be treated in somewhat greater detail. The essential facts have been known for some time and only need to be recapitulated, although the interpretation given here varies very considerably from the accepted view. In a detailed letter to Stalin in October, Ribbentrop had advocated co-operation with the Soviet Union and proposed that Molotov should come to Berlin to discuss the points at issue between them.[150] Stalin accepted the invitation and on the morning of 12 November 1940 his Foreign Minister arrived at the Anhalter Station.

The discussions commenced without delay. At first Molotov conferred with Ribbentrop, who repeated his familiar themes: Britain was already beaten, and it was only a matter of time before she admitted it. Then the German Foreign Minister sought to obtain an agreement from his opposite number to a definition of the borders between the Soviet and the Axis Powers' spheres of interest in Europe and Africa, and also between the Soviet and Japanese spheres of interest in the Far East, where the Japanese were laying claim to a 'Great East Asia' region. He also urged Molotov to contemplate expansion to the south – in the direction of the Persian Gulf and the Arabian Sea – with an unmistakable reference to India. The object of this was to tempt the Kremlin with a share of the booty available after the predicted bankruptcy of the British Empire, and also to divert its attention away from Europe and get it mixed up in a conflict with the British and possibly with the Americans. In this manner, the Soviet Union was to be integrated into the Three Power Pact and become part of the 'continental block'. The Soviets, however, had their sights set on a different continental bloc, one where they would no longer be sandwiched between Germany and Japan.

The discussion between Molotov and Hitler which followed revolved around the same topics. The Führer made a number of general observations, but sought in particular to justify his policy in the Balkans and Finland by saying that the necessities of war had forced his hand. In the struggle against Great Britain, Germany was compelled to press forward into regions in which it had no real political or economic interest. The dictator then let slip the remark that Germany was engaged in a life-and-death struggle with Britain,[151] which elicited from Molotov the scornful quip that obviously Germany was fighting for her life and

Britain for her death.[152] The question is this: did Hitler merely use that sentence to make his policy sound more acceptable to his guest, or was it a genuine mistake which unwittingly betrayed his real assessment of the war situation?

Whereas Hitler and Ribbentrop adopted a friendly attitude, Molotov was very reserved; and while the Germans often wandered off the subject, making nebulous observations, Molotov's mode of speech and argument seemed 'mathematically precise and unswervingly logical'.[153] Ignoring the plans for dividing up the world which he had just heard, Stalin's ambassador put concrete questions and demands which referred to precisely those points where Soviet expansionist policy had come up against German resistance, or would come up against it in the future. In line with the agreement of 1939, he first demanded that Finland be handed over, then expressed his displeasure at the German guarantee to Rumania and wanted to know Germany's attitude regarding a similar Soviet guarantee to Bulgaria; a further demand referred to bases in the region of the Dardanelles. The Foreign Minister also wanted more details about the Three Power Pact and the 'Great East Asia' region. 'The questions rained down on Hitler's head. None of the foreign visitors had spoken to him like this in my presence',[154] reported the chief interpreter Paul Schmidt. This time, however, the dictator did not react with one of his fits of temper, but was gentleness and politeness itself.[155] The only time Molotov expressed agreement was when the Führer declared that the U.S.A. had no business interfering in the affairs of Europe, Africa or Asia.

In addition to all this, Molotov left no grounds for doubting that the borders separating off the different spheres of interest decided upon the previous year could only be regarded as a partial solution, which had been overtaken by what had happened since. The agreement of 1939 had referred to a distinct stage which had come to an end with the conclusion of the Polish campaign; the second stage had ended with the campaign in France; now it was time for the third stage.[156] Molotov hinted at how he imagined this third stage – and possible further stages to follow – in his final conversation with Ribbentrop in the Foreign Ministry's air raid shelter on the evening of 13 November. Here he not only re-emphasised the demands already made relating to Finland, Bulgaria and the Turkish Straits, but also declared his country's interest in Rumania, Hungary, Yugoslavia and Greece – in other words the whole of south-east Europe. Scarcely less perturbing was the reminder he gave of the protocol dealing with the future configuration of Poland, agreed upon by Germany and the Soviet Union, and the suggestion that an exchange of opinion on this would be necessary to put it into practice. The subject of Swedish neutrality was also broached, as was the question of the sea passages out of the Baltic (Big Belt, Little Belt, Sund, Kattegat and Skagerrak). The Soviet government believed that discussion of these points was necessary, along the lines of those in progress at the time regarding the Danube Commissions – in other words with Moscow claiming the dominant position.[157] These enormous demands have been accurately described as follows:

> Russia is getting ready to turn the Baltic into a Russian inland sea, to subjugate the Balkans, to regulate Polish conditions in such a manner that, if possible, the fourth division of Poland of August and September 1939 can be replaced by a kind of Polish congress under Russian sovereignty.[158]

Ribbentrop's last, almost imploring question as to whether the Kremlin was attracted by the idea of securing territories leading to the Indian Ocean received no answer from Molotov.

Next morning the Foreign Minister's special train left the Anhalter Station in Berlin. One of the most important events of the Second World War, perhaps even of this century, was at an end.

It was a kind of epilogue when the written conditions for Soviet entry into the Three Power Pact were handed over to the German ambassador in Moscow a few days later. Nothing of the contents had changed. In Stalin's opinion, the German troops had first to be withdrawn from Finland, Bulgaria must be included in the Soviet safety zone, and a Soviet military base should be established at the Dardanelles. If Turkey were to offer resistance, then joint military and diplomatic measures from Germany, Italy and the Soviet Union were demanded.[159] Thus it was expected that if necessary the Axis powers would offer armed assistance for the furtherance of these exclusively Soviet claims.

All this was unacceptable to Germany. To pull out of Finland would have meant losing an important strategic position and making the vital nickel and timber supplies a hostage to Soviet goodwill. The conditions regarding Bulgaria were unacceptable – firstly because Hitler might need to use this country as a deployment area against the Greeks or British, and secondly – and more importantly – because a Soviet military presence there would have been a threat from the south to Rumania, which for military and economic reasons was indispensable to Germany. Furthermore, on the basis of his previous experiences and Molotov's candid statement, Hitler had every reason to fear that as soon as their present wishes were granted the Soviets would be making new and even more dangerous demands. There could be no doubt that the

Kremlin was applying to Germany the very strategy which Hitler had practised so long and so successfully – namely, to extort concessions in order to gain a more favourable vantage point for further extortion, and thus step by step to completely subjugate the victim. The Soviet encroachment into Finland and Bulgaria was dangerous enough, but Molotov's further extravagant claims amounted to nothing less than an encircling movement from Poland and the Balkans – one which would have made a successful defence against attack from the east impossible, and which would reduce Germany's role from representative to satellite. What Stalin's ambassador had handed over was certainly not an ultimatum with a time limit, but it was a scarcely disguised summons, a demand for submission.

In such a situation not only Hitler but any head of state would have considered ways of breaking the stranglehold in due time. In any case, Hitler's intentions regarding an armed attack on the Soviets were considerably strengthened. On 18 December 1940 he issued his historic 'Instruction No. 21' about Operation Barbarossa:

> The German Army must be ready, even before the end of the war with England, to crush Russia in a rapid campaign.

Whether Hitler would have attacked if the discussions with Moscow had taken a different course must remain open to question. In 'Instruction No. 18' Hitler had reserved this military option for himself, irrespective of the outcome of the talks. In any case, if the Soviet Union did join the Three Power Pact then Germany would be dependent on the Kremlin's loyalty to the agreed terms, which would have meant a further element of uncertainty. Now, however, Molotov had let the cat out of the bag and had dispelled all doubts about Moscow's intentions. Germany had a choice: to submit or to fight.

Molotov's bluntness has sometimes been criticised as a bad mistake which unwittingly provoked the German attack. If this was the case then it does seem scarcely comprehensible that such a reserved politician, precise and calculating in his thoughts, could have committed such a blunder. This was the opinion of Gafencu, but his only knowledge of the Berlin negotiations came from Hitler's account in his speech of 22 June 1941. He considered it 'very improbable that Molotov, who was justifiably thought to be clever and secretive, should have opened his heart in this way to such a dangerous opponent'.[160] For this reason he believed that Hitler had lied, or at least given a very distorted version of the meeting; but the documents which became available after the end of the war revealed that this was not the case. The matter now became even more puzzling. In the opinion of Byrnes, the U.S. Foreign

Minister at the time, these discussions were highly significant and led to a turning point in the war. Stalin's ambassador, he believed, had overshot the mark and, especially in his discussions with Hitler on 13 November 1940, had made a serious diplomatic blunder.[161] David Irving also wonders whether anyone will ever fathom what caused Molotov to be so frank at this time. The correct interpretation, however, may be found in E. Hughes:

> Although Hitler recognised Russia's conquests and spheres of interest in the Middle East and in the Baltic countries to an extent which went far beyond all Russian aspirations since Peter the Great and up to Alexander Isvolski, Molotov curtly demanded further concessions in the Balkan area and the Dardanelles, fully knowing that this would enrage the Führer and so lure him to declare war on Russia. The plan was a success and on 21 June 1941 Hitler started his fateful attack.[162]

Finally Hillgruber (see page 8), in attempting to fathom Moscow's long-term aims, finds himself unable to decide whether the attack was caused by a blunder almost unique in world history on the part of the usually taciturn Foreign Minister, or whether it was the result of a specially refined tactical manoeuvre which the historian would find hard to understand.

Weighing these different interpretations in the balance, Molotov's outspokenness doesn't appear to be a blunder, but a precisely calculated component of a political and strategic master plan, involving an undeniably grandiose conception and carried out with highly sophisticated tactics. If this has gone largely unnoticed up to the present, it is possibly because Molotov's behaviour has been interpreted by examining its consequences but not its hypotheses. In November 1940 he certainly had not anticipated the successes of the German army. On the contrary, his tough and confident behaviour expressed the conviction that when the time came the Soviet army would be able to defeat the Wehrmacht without any serious difficulty. It was false judgement in the *military* sphere rather than the *political* sphere that led to the miscalculation, and which prevented the ambitious plans of the Soviet leaders from being more than partially successful.

It must again be emphasised that it is not possible to obtain documentary evidence of Stalin's strategic master plan For this to succeed, complete discretion was required. What was being planned was never put down in writing. It was neither documented nor talked about. It was simply put into practice. However, in the light of certain political, psychological and strategic considerations, with the help of certain clues, and especially by examining the actual behaviour of the Soviet leaders it is possible to be confident of revealing their intentions with a fair degree of accuracy, and to understand their tactical moves – even, if need be, their silence.

It has already been mentioned that for the Soviets the main problem was not a military one, for an early victory was expected. The contentious issue was how to gain the most favourable political and psychological position for the planned attack – against the Germans, who were to be crushed, against the British and Americans, who were to be overwhelmed, and in relation to their own people, whose zeal for war had to be aroused. It would be most advantageous from the point of view of all three if Hitler were to attack; and if he would not do so of his own accord, then he had to be provoked – but secretly, so that the Soviet Union could appear in the eyes of the world as the victim of an unjustifiable act of aggression.

If we accept these assumptions then an aura of mathematical precision and unswerving logicality surrounds the position taken by Molotov and the way he presented it, indeed his whole demeanour in Berlin. In Moscow the date of the journey had been carefully chosen and the situation in Germany precisely analysed. As the whole plan depended on no agreement being reached between Hitler and Britain and America, the Kremlin waited for the result of the U.S. presidential elections, which removed all worries in this connection. The Kremlin was also fully aware of the fact that since the early summer the situation of the Axis powers had greatly deteriorated: the air battle over England was lost and London could now rely on increased American aid; to all intents and purposes the negotiations with Pétain and Franco had yielded no results; and after Italy's defeats at the hands of the British the debacle in the mountains on the Greek border began to loom large. It is also probable that Soviet intelligence had learnt something about the uncertainty in German military planning and the confusion in its armaments industry. Furthermore, Germany's economic situation was not favourable: Hitler had indeed conquered many lands and brought them under his influence, but the regions he controlled were not self-sufficient – they had to be supplied, and the English navy was guarding the sea crossings. Germany's economic dependence on the Soviet Union had hardly decreased, perhaps it had even increased, so Molotov could be sure, in the economic sphere, of holding all the trump cards in his hand. He hadn't the slightest reason for accepting German pleas to join a continental bloc.

Stalin and his ambassador would certainly have considered the range of possible German reactions to their demands. If Hitler made only partial concessions the Soviet Union would win a new victory, without risk and without bloodshed, and gain a stronger position for any future armed struggle. If he made no move the Kremlin, with the Red Army at its back, could at any time become more importunate in its demands. The third possibility was that the Germans would attack. If in doing so they wanted to avoid a war on two fronts, they would have to strike before the British and Americans won a foothold on the continent – which fitted in perfectly with Kremlin thinking since by then the Soviet Union intended to have both the 'German problem' and the 'European problem' settled once and for all.

A German attack suited Soviet interests in another respect, and although it involved some risk from the military point of view, it was not deemed unacceptable. By the spring of 1941 – such was the conviction of Moscow – the Red Army would have progressed so far in its preparations that it would be supremely capable of meeting all eventualities. The risk of defeat was negligible when compared with the considerable, even decisive, political and psychological advantages to be had. Germany would have to bear the odium of the 'treaty breaker' and, as in Poland, the aggressor. The Soviet people, feeling themselves victims of a malicious attack, would wage in holy anger the 'most just war in the history of mankind', and in the end break through and destroy the aggressor on his own territory. Moreover, a German attack would enable the Soviets to gain a favourable position in relation to Britain and the U.S.A. If the Kremlin wanted to take the initiative it could either come to an agreement with London (or Washington) first, or it could begin a war against Germany without such an agreement. But negotiations were not in the Soviet interest, for in the course of these unpleasant questions could be expected – concerning Poland, the Baltic states, Finland, the Danube Commission, and especially Soviet intentions for the future. This would make it more difficult to present the Western powers with a *fait accompli*. A Soviet attack on Germany without a previous agreement would certainly be welcomed because it would lighten the burden on the West; but it could also have raised suspicions regarding Moscow's aims, and there was nothing the Kremlin feared more than an agreement between Berlin and London.

It would be much more favourable if Hitler were to start the hostilities. Not only would Germany be held responsible for the ensuing conflict, but the Kremlin would also be able to conceal its intentions much more effectively, representing the victorious advance as a reaction to the German attack. Additionally, such an attack would help to create a political and psychological myth, which Stalin knew very well could be worth more than whole armies. If the 'Fatherland of all Workers' could be portrayed to the world as the victim of a cunning attack, public opinion – especially in Britain and the U.S.A. – could be mobilised by goodwill campaigns, which in their turn could exert pressure on political leaders. If a British or American politician were to speak out against offering help to the Soviet people, or even speak in favour of seeking an understanding with the aggressor, then the mass of workers would sweep him aside in a storm of indignation. In its essentials, this is what subsequently happened.

> What finally determined the attitude of the U.S.A. and England was the consistent support given to the righteous struggle of the Soviet people by the broad mass of the people, together with the powerful impetus of the movement demanding active assistance for the Soviet Union. Whatever selfish actions and reactionary aims the governments of the capitalist lands pursued and however hostile they were towards socialism, they were forced to support the Soviet Union because of the pressure exerted by the broad mass of the people, and in view of the political situation.[163]

Although this description gives the one-sided Soviet standpoint, there really was such a movement and it really did exert considerable influence.

If all these things are considered, Molotov's behaviour in Berlin appears as part of a well-conceived and far-sighted project. He refused to react to the nebulous thoughts and suggestions of his treaty partners, but concentrated completely on the points at issue in order to exacerbate the conflict. By his ominous revelations in the air raid shelter he impressed upon the Germans, with the utmost bluntness, that they had to choose either to fight or to give in to Soviet wishes, and by making this challenge he hoped to provoke them into an attack. In this he was successful. It is not at all surprising that the Soviets maintain a persistent silence about these events to this day.

The Stage Is Set

With Molotov's visit and the confirmation in writing of the Soviet conditions for entry into the Three Power Pact – which incidentally received no reply from Hitler – the stage was set for the main events of the great drama that was to follow. Anything else that happened in Europe between then and the day Barbarossa was launched would no longer seem important.

Hitler devoted all his attention towards bringing south-east Europe under his control. The first to be subjugated were the Hungarians, who joined the Three Power Pact on 20 November 1940, to be followed by Rumania and Czechoslovakia. Although these moves were directed against the Soviets, their expressions of annoyance were moderate, which in some cases was misunderstood as a sign of weakness.[164] In fact, this apparent docility was simply an element in the double game Moscow was conducting. Behind the scenes Germany had suffered extreme provocation at the hands of Moscow; in public the Soviet leaders endeavoured to avoid any semblance of antagonising Hitler and to display their love of peace for all to see. In line with this *Pravda* published on 31 December 1940 a review of the year which boasted:

> Our country is persistently following its policy of peace and neutrality; it is exploiting all the advantages of this peace and is successfully putting into practice its great plans for reconstructing and organising the economy.[165]

Gafencu made the following comment:

> This pacifist demagogy, chosen for use at home and abroad, had also a further aim: to make the secretly provoked German attack appear all the more contemptible when viewed in the shining light of the Soviet love of peace.

However, in the spring of 1941 the dissension between the two countries became more pronounced: first in the case of Bulgaria – regarded by the Soviets as part of their safety zone but needed by Hitler as a springboard for military intervention in Greece, where the British had established themselves after the Italian attack. This action had brought the Rumanian oilfields within the range of British bombers, which was a threat the Führer could not tolerate. Consequently the first months of the new year saw a bitter diplomatic struggle over Sofia, which ended in favour of Germany. However, when Bulgaria joined the Three Power Pact and on 2 March 1941 German troops from Rumania crossed over the Danube to the south, the Kremlin protested much more vehemently than in the past, though still without threatening any definite sanctions.

Even when tension became more acute over Yugoslavia the Kremlin displayed astonishing forbearance. After prolonged hesitation the government in Belgrade had yielded to German pressure and joined the Three Power Pact on 25 March 1941; but shortly afterwards anti-German forces under General Simovic staged a minor revolt, in which the Soviet Union was suspected of playing a part. In any case, Stalin concluded a pact of non-aggression and friendship with the new government, although its terms were so framed that it left Moscow with few obligations. The main purpose of the agreement was to record Soviet interest in Yugoslavia and to warn Hitler not to undertake an attack; it also represented the bare minimum of what the Soviet Union needed to do in public in order to counter any accusations of treachery towards its Slav brothers. But in confidential conversations Stalin was not so reticent. When the Yugoslavian Ambassador asked him, 'And what if the Germans get annoyed and attack you?' he answered cheerfully and quite unmoved, 'Just let them come!'

Meanwhile Stalin had brought the military into the Soviet political arena. Schukov became a candidate for the Central Committee, and in all the military and arms manufacturers composed twenty-one per cent of Central Committee membership by the beginning of 1941. After the Eighteenth Party Congress war preparations went ahead at full speed. On 8 March 1941 Defence Minister Timoschenko divided up the responsibilities so that Chief of the General Staff Schukov held more responsibility than his predecessors: he was put in charge of the administration of the intelligence service, fuel supplies and air defences; he also had control over the two most important training establishments for senior command personel – the General Staff Academy and the Frunse War Academy. In April 1941 Timoschenko ordered that the backbone of the Red Army, the Infantry divisions, were to be put on a war footing. This was only partly carried out.[166]

Hitler was by then no longer master of his situation. Owing to Mussolini's absurd and self-willed attack on Greece, the Führer found himself in a critical position. If he wanted to defend the Rumanian oilfields and save his partner from catastrophe, then he had to take military action. Accordingly on 6 April 1941 the German army went into action once more. Another successful *Blitzkrieg* ensued. A few weeks later Yugoslavia and Greece were forced to capitulate and the British were driven from the Balkans – an eventuality which was far from displeasing to the Kremlin (see page 65) This Balkan campaign was an important military achievement, especially in view of the problem of supplying the army and the difficulties posed by the terrain, but it cut across Hitler's main plan by forcing him to postpone Operation Barbarossa from mid-May to the end of June. Opinions vary as to the effect of this postponement on the invasion, but it is worth bearing in mind that very bad weather conditions prevailed in the field of operations during these weeks, with flooded rivers and roads deep in mud, and this alone would probably have made a postponement necessary.

During the German advance into the Balkans Moscow did more than just keep silent: it switched over to an attitude of loyalty, indeed of friendship, towards Berlin – probably in order to gain time and conceal its real intentions. The famous scene which took place on the platform of the Moscow railway station fits into the pattern of these efforts: the Japanese Foreign Minister was returning home on 4 April 1941 after signing the neutrality pact with the Soviet Union when Stalin and Molotov appeared quite unexpectedly to see him off. What then happened – in the presence of the diplomatic corps – is related by the German Ambassador at the time, Graf Schulenberg:

> It was obvious that Stalin was looking for me, for as soon as he saw me he came up, put his arm round my shoulders and said: 'We must remain friends, and you must do everything to keep this so'. Somewhat later Stalin turned to the German Deputy Military Attaché, Colonel Krebs, first made certain that he was German, then said to him, 'We will remain friends with you, in any case.' There is no doubt that Stalin greeted myself and Colonel Krebs deliberately to create a situation which would be noticed by the many people present.[167]

But these assertions of friendship had a hollow ring. When, contrary to his usual habits, Stalin made any demonstrative appearance in public, there were always significance reasons for him doing so, and if one considers the background to that theatrically sentimental scene then it seems to assume an almost Shakespearian character. While the sly Georgian was embracing the Germans in public, he had just covered his rear for the war against Germany; and while he was honouring Matsuoka by appearing personally to see him off, he had encouraged Japan to make the most fateful mistake in its history.

It had taken quite some time to arrive at the neutrality pact with Japan. As a result of suffering many defeats in clashes with the Red Army, and because of the erosion of its alliance with Germany through the Hitler–Stalin Pact, Japan had got into a very unfavourable situation and was attempting to improve its relations with the Soviet Union, efforts which were also supported by Berlin. However, a dispute about Japanese prospecting rights in North Sakhalin had brought these negotiations to a dead end, and in April 1941 they seemed close to failure, before the personal intervention of Stalin led to the signing of the neutrality pact. It is worth noting that the wording of this pact was such that – according to one possible interpretation – the Japanese would be obliged to observe neutrality even in the case of a Soviet attack against Germany,[168] as were the Russians in the event of a Japanese action in the Pacific. Stalin was, of course, seeking to secure his rear before the collision with Germany, but he was perhaps also pursuing other more important aims.

He gave a strong hint of this in a toast after the signing of the pact: 'Doesn't this [the conclusion of the treaty] enable Japan to make advances to the south without any fear?'[169] By this suggestion – which incidentally fitted in with German plans for a continental bloc – the Japanese policy of expansion was to be diverted away from the Soviet Union and towards British and U.S. interests to the south. Stalin's astute move soon brought about the desired result. Directly after the signing of the pact and encouraged by the fact that an agreement had been reached, the Japanese army and navy began to intensify their expansion to the south, in order to improve the nation's strategic position and its supply of raw materials, and also to put pressure on the Chinese from this direction. They were prepared to face the consequences if this action resulted in a clash with Britain and the U.S.A.[170]

Stalin's plans went further, however, as Grigore Gafencu has pointed out with particular clarity: Japanese penetration to the south would free eastern Siberia from the Japanese threat, relieve China, which was finding it difficult to breathe in the stranglehold exerted by Tokyo, and involve Japan in a war with the U.S.A. In the long run, this would spell disaster for Japan, but it would also reveal the weakness of the British Empire, strengthen the nationalist feeling of the broad mass of the people in central Asia, and further Asia's fight for freedom.[171]

Just as the pact with Hitler was to unleash the 'imperialist war' in the west, so the neutrality pact with Japan would serve the same purpose in Asia. The Kremlin hoped that the bitter struggles between Britain, the U.S.A. and Japan would anger and arouse the mass of the people in Asia and so make them ripe for a revolution under Soviet leadership.

The neutrality pact therefore formed an integral part of Stalin's broad strategy of diverting the expansionist policies of the 'aggressive' capitalist powers away from the Soviet Union and on to the 'non-aggressive' powers, which were much more important opponents in the long run. It was intended that if this failed to unleash the 'imperialist war' and bring revolution, it would at least bring further decisive advantages to the Soviet Union. Having already succeeded in entangling Hitler in a kind of proxy war with the Western democracies by agreeing not to engage him in the east, it was now intended to offer similar protection to the Japanese in order to entice them into a confrontation with the British and Americans. In this manner, and once again using a neutrality pact, another potential attacker was made into an instrument of Soviet interests and used against the capitalist states. Needless to say it was of special significance to the Soviet leaders that as many as possible of British and U.S. armed forces should be tied down in the Far East, while they themselves were laying hands on Germany and Europe.

This pact also offers a fresh example of the Soviets' tactic of imputing to others what they themselves were doing. Just as the Hitler–Stalin Pact was justified by alleging that it was the intention of the Western powers to provoke Germany into a war with the Soviet Union, it was now asserted that this neutrality agreement had thwarted Washington's dark plans to entangle Japan in a military confrontation with the Red Army.[172] Quite apart from the fact that there was no plausible evidence – let alone proof – of such a plan, it would have been directly opposed to U.S. interests. The might of the Soviet Union was greatly underestimated in Washington, where it was thought that the Red Army would be unable to withstand an attack by a great power for long. This would mean that at the most all the British and Americans would expect from a war between the Three Power Pact and the Soviet Union was some short-term relief, whereas the final result would be catastrophic: a continental bloc from Brittany to Kamchatka under German–Japanese dominance.

During the last months before the great collision the duplicity of the Kremlin's German policy became more and more obvious. Outwardly the Soviet leaders made a most striking display of their loyalty, even though behind the scenes the psychological and military preparations for war were being pursued with great impetus.

For example, the Soviets moderated their pressure on Finland and Rumania, dismissed the diplomatic representatives of Belgium, Norway, Greece and Yugoslavia – on the grounds that these states had lost their sovereignty – and sent an ambassador to the Vichy government in France. When revolutionary forces in Iraq, fighting against the British, founded a government friendly to Germany under Raschid Ali el Ghailani, it was at once recognised by Moscow. In addition, supplies to Germany, which had suffered delays at the beginning of the year, were now considerably accelerated and extended, and on 12 April an oil agreement favourable to Germany was concluded.[173]

Today these and similar measures are mostly considered to be nothing more than tactical, time-saving manoeuvres, for which good reasons can be produced. Possibly the speedy German victory in the difficult terrain of the Balkans had aroused some doubts about the dogma of the 'easy victory', and probably it was also recognised that in spite of strenuous efforts the war preparations were proceeding more slowly than expected. Competent military experts expressed their doubts about coping with the momentous situation looming before them. On 23 February 1941, on Red Army Day, Schukov stated in *Pravda* that the armed forces were engaged in a transformation which hadn't yet been completed and that they were a long way from achieving their goals.[174] In view of the gigantic rearmament programme already mentioned (page 74) these statements are doubtless accurate, but Schukov also emphasised that the Red Army had made considerable progress. Nevertheless, some postponement of the armed conflict must have seemed desirable from the military point of view.

There is also evidence to suggest that the Soviet government's declarations of loyalty were not merely meant to win time. It is generally known that in the summer of 1941 the Kremlin was very well informed – through foreign and also Soviet sources – of German plans.[175] For example, on 20 March General Golikov, head of the military secret service, made a fairly detailed and accurate report about German preparations and intentions; and at the beginning of May the People's Commissar of the navy sent Stalin a memorandum with similar information. Yet both came to the completely illogical conclusion – but in their opinion one which Stalin would want to hear – that these were all rumours or false reports disseminated by foreign intelligence services in order to harm the Soviet Union.[176]

If Stalin adhered firmly to the myth of German treachery towards the peace-loving and trusting Soviet Union in his relations with very senior officials, he took even greater pains to do so with outsiders. This was made abundantly clear in various propaganda and diplomatic moves during the last weeks before the war started. On 9 May the Moscow news agency Tass denied rumours about Soviet troop concentrations on the Western border, and on 13 June *Izvestiya* once again denied all similar rumours as well as reports about alleged disputes between the U.S.S.R. and Germany, saying that these were all inventions dreamed up by enemies of Germany and the Soviet Union. Reports of Germany's intention to attack the Soviet Union couldn't possibly be correct, and German troop movements from the Balkans to the east and north-east borders of the German empire had nothing to do with German–Soviet relations. Both powers were sticking to their agreements and that was how it would remain. In fact, just a few hours before the German army attacked, Molotov invited the German ambassador once again into the Kremlin and informed him that a number of circumstances gave the impression that the German government was dissatisfied with the Soviet government, and that there were even rumours abroad about preparations being made for a war between the two nations. The Soviet government couldn't explain the reason for German dissatisfaction and would like to know the reason for the present position of German–Soviet relations.[177] Had Molotov forgotten what he had said seven months previously in Berlin? When Ambassador von der Schulenburg handed over to him the declaration of war simultaneously with the start of the German advance, the Foreign Minister didn't bat an eyelid, but maintained his sang-froid and asked his opposite number: 'Do you believe that we have deserved this?'

Whether during those last months the Kremlin hoped to gain time by this ostensible display of friendship towards Germany is open to dispute. It was probably more designed to make the perfidiousness of the German attack contrast all the more strongly with the background of Russian loyalty, and so to camouflage Stalin's own imperialist intentions regarding the British and Americans. This stratagem of psychological warfare was to have a much more convincing effect later on as a result of the remarkable success of the German army at the beginning of the invasion. Even Churchill failed to see through it – he wrote in his memoirs after the war that 'Stalin and his commissars were the most outwitted bunglers of the Second World War'.[178] The real bunglers were not in Moscow at the time.

But however much the Kremlin's campaign of psychological warfare was intent on spreading the myth of the treacherous attack during those fateful months, it had also to pursue other goals which at times had a contrary effect. The hatred of the conqueror had to be stirred up and exploited in the regions occupied by Hitler, so that the Red Army could pose more credibly as liberators when the time came. It was also necessary to make Soviet policies, which were at times hard to understand, plausible to communists and other supporters abroad. The Soviet people themselves, and especially the armed forces, had to be prepared for the conflict with Germany. During the last weeks of peace this often produced that peculiar atmosphere described in Simonov's novel *The Living and the Dead*: 'Everyone had been expecting war, but when it broke out it was like a flash of lightning from a clear sky'.[179]

In the terms of Comintern propaganda the war was 'imperialist' and therefore 'unjust', but in spite of that its support for Germany up to the collapse of France had been quite unmistakable. Yet from July 1940 a change had begun to make itself felt. First and foremost, the Treaty of Compiègne was criticised. In this case the complaint was expressed through the medium of the German emigrés in Stockholm who, ten days after the armistice was signed, summoned all workers to fight against the subjection of French workers and the imperialist enslavement enforced by the dictates of the German bourgeoisie.[180] At the beginning of August a newspaper in Riga, now communist, published an article along similar lines, which led to a complaint by Ribbentrop to the Soviet Ambassador.[181] These anti-German utterances were sometimes accompanied by even sharper attacks on the British (or Americans), and the peoples of the occupied territories were warned not to expect any deliverance from these 'imperialists'.[182] It thus proved possible to be very articulate without betraying any true intentions.

Meanwhile, anti-German propaganda in the Red Army, which had not been abandoned even when German–Soviet friendship was at its height, was noticeably increased.[183] On 1 May Marshal Timoschenko issued an order of the day which stated:

> The Red Army has augmented its experience of war and is ready to offer annihilating resistance to any imperialist blow against the interests of our Soviet state or our Soviet people.[184]

In view of the situation at the time, it was not hard to guess who was expected to deliver such a blow.

The Soviets therefore made ready for an early confrontation with Germany, whether Hitler attacked or they themselves had to make the first move, and deployed the Red Army accordingly. The offensive character of the Soviet military will be demonstrated later (page 104) but first some misinterpretations of Soviet plans need to be corrected. In keeping with the original intentions of the Kremlin and by reference to a series of relevant Soviet documents it is sometimes asserted that in 1941 Moscow wanted to await the last phase of the 'imperialist war' and only then bring the Red Army into play.[185] Another version suggests that the Red Army had been made ready to attack Germany while the Wehrmacht was engaged in an invasion of England. Both interpretations are unconvincing. At the time, with the U.S.A. still neutral, the last phase of the war was a long way off, and a cross-Channel invasion had become extremely improbable because the prerequisite for success – mastery of the air in the area of operations – had turned out to be beyond Hitler's power following defeat in the Battle of Britain in the late summer of 1940. Since then Britain's defence capabilities, with U.S. aid, were being strengthened month by month. The enormous increase in Soviet armed forces, much of it due to increased support from the armaments industry and the war economy, was now concentrated in the west of the nation, which suggests that the Kremlin was counting on an outbreak of hostilities in the near future, come what may.

This assumption is also confirmed by Stalin's own behaviour at the time. On 5 May 1941 he delivered a forty-minute speech at a passing out parade of cadets at the Military Academy, the text of which was unfortunately not made public. On the next day *Pravda* made a short report of this under the heading 'We must be ready for any surprise', stating how Stalin had emphasised that, in accordance with the demands of modern warfare, the army had been reorganised and to a large extent re-equipped.[186] There are various versions of the contents of the speech, but they all agree that the Soviet dictator was of the opinion that war was imminent and would 'almost inevitably' be fought out in 1942, in which case the Soviets would have to take the initiative.[187] The account given by Gustav Hilger, German Ambassador in Moscow at the time (and incidentally an advocate of reaching an understanding with the Soviet Union, as was also Ambassador von der Schulenburg), is noteworthy. Hilger reports that the embassy received information according to which Stalin had recommended a compromise with Germany in his speech to the Military Academy.

> In flagrant contradiction of this are the accounts given to me during the war by three high-ranking Russian officers, prisoners of war, who had been present at the banquet. According to them the head of the academy, Lieutenant-General Chosin, had wanted to propose a toast to the peaceful policies of the Soviet Union – to which Stalin reacted with sharp disapproval, saying that it was time to drop this defensive attitude because it was out of date. Admittedly this attitude had helped to push the borders of the Soviet Union well forward in the west and north, increasing its population by thirteen millions in the process, but now not another foot of ground could be gained with such peaceful sentiments. The Red Army must get used to the idea that the era of the peace policy was finished and the era of a violent extension of the socialist front had dawned. Anyone who failed to recognise the necessity of offensive action was a bourgeois and a fool. It was also time to put an end, once and for all, to the adulation of the German Army.[188]

Hilger explains the contradiction between the two reports by saying that there was intentional disinformation from the Soviet authorities.

The correctness of the officers' statements is confirmed by the fact that

100

their accounts agree almost word for word, even though they had had no contact with each other. One is therefore very inclined to believe that Stalin intentionally let the first report be passed into the hands of the embassy in order to give Hitler proof of his peaceful intentions.[189]

Far more important than this disinformation, which only follows an established pattern, is Stalin's well-substantiated statement that the collision with Germany would happen 'almost unavoidably' in the year 1942, unless it was set in motion earlier by a German attack. The date given is a further important clue as to Stalin's intentions. The last phase of the war was certainly not to be expected in the near future and a German attempt to land in England was, as we have seen, an impossibility. Yet Stalin could certainly rely on the fact that by 1942 he would be much better armed and still in a position to present the British and Americans with a *fait accompli* in Europe. If, however, he had to hang on much longer, the war potential of the U.S.A. would start playing an increasingly decisive role.

If the above assumptions are correct then another circumstance which has long puzzled historians becomes comprehensible. On 7 May 1941, two days after his speech to the officers, Stalin became President of the Council of People's Commissars. Up to then this office had been held by Molotov, who was now demoted to Vice President, but still kept his position in the Foreign Office. The importance of these moves was recognised everywhere, though the meaning behind them was not clearly understood. Gafencu, at the time still Rumanian Ambassador in Moscow, wrote later about this:

> The appearance of Stalin at the head of the government could only mean one thing: in the hour of danger, the captain of the ship was climbing onto the bridge. The man who up to then had fulfilled all the tasks of power now took upon himself, at a moment of extraordinary crisis, all the responsibilities and all the dangers.[190]

This verdict is basically correct, but was nonetheless distorted by the events of the summer and autumn of 1941. Certainly Stalin would have liked more time to complete his rearmament, and he was certainly not fully prepared for the approaching conflict; but it is likely that he still expected his armed forces, in spite of a number of remaining deficiencies, to be capable even in 1941 of throwing back a German attack, subjugating the German army and so forcing open the door to Europe at last. Full of such expectations, Stalin no longer wanted to exercise his power in the background, as hitherto, but to stand before all the world and glory in his victory, while the unconquerable Red Army, amidst roars of applause from the liberated masses, completed its triumphal march to the Atlantic.

Of course, things turned out differently. It is well known that during the first days of the war Stalin was completely confused and only on 3 July with his historic speech over the radio did he again make his presence felt in public. This deep depression is sometimes attributed to the moral shock occasioned by Hitler's perfidious breach of faith; it seems more realistic to attribute any such shock to the unexpected defeats. But possibly there were other reasons; the mirage of a speedy victory was disappearing into nothing under the hammer-blows of the Wehrmacht, and instead of the glory of victory, there was now only the prospect of a struggle for survival.

In Germany, too, they believed victory would be easy – or at least indulged in wishful thinking on this score. In fact, opinions regarding the prospects of success in the eastern campaign had a peculiarly hollow ring. On the surface, there was an excess of optimism, but deep down there was gnawing worry and uncertainty.

Hitler and his generals, as well as the general staffs of the Western powers, had a fairly poor opinion of the fighting efficiency of the Red Army, which though numerically strong was badly equipped, technically out of date and had lost most of its capable leaders in the great purges of 1937–38. The Soviet troops, whom the Germans had come across in Poland, had made a very bad impression; and the Winter War against Finland seemed once again to have confirmed the generally low opinion of the Soviet fighting forces. The Germans, of course, were not without ideological dogmas of their own, and believed both in the demoralising effect of Bolshevism and in the ethnic inferiority of the Soviet people. Furthermore, the spectacular success of previous campaigns had given the German army an exaggerated opinion of its abilities, making them think that under the leadership of the genius Hitler, 'the greatest general of all time', nothing was impossible. The dictator and his General Staff believed they could destroy the main enemy forces near the border and then, without any serious difficulties, occupy the greater part of European Russia together with the oilfields of Baku.

Additionally, as a result of the impenetrable Soviet veil of secrecy the Germans knew so little about their opponents that Albert Seaton gave his chapter on the subject the title 'The Enemy: the Unknown Quantity'.[191] For example, the secret handbook about the fighting forces of the U.S.S.R., published on 1 January 1941 by the Foreign Army East department, had to admit that there were substantial gaps in the information about the Red Army. With regard to Soviet industrial potential, the Germans were dependent on very rough estimates which were far removed from reality – the capacity and efficiency of the new industrial area in the Urals and Siberia remained hidden from them. The possibilities of obtaining information were better only in the western regions of the Soviet Union which had only recently been occupied; aerial reconnaissance also yielded many important results.[192]

In spite of all this, Hitler and his accomplices embarked on the infamous and staggeringly ambitious plan to desolate the Soviet Union and to enslave its people. The Jews, in particular, and the communist intelligentsia were to be physically exterminated. Many officers brought up in the traditions of chivalrous warfare condemned such orders, and in some cases opposed them by passive resistance, but that was all. Having said that, their opponents often acted with frightening cruelty and it must not be forgotten that Hitler's 'racial war of annihilation' had not only a predecessor but also probably a model in Stalin's 'class war' campaigns of annihilation against the bourgeoisie and the kulaks.

However, in his heart of hearts not even Hitler was so sure of victory; and there was no lack of warning voices – even allowing that many people claimed to have warned of the catastrophe in advance only after it had occurred. In particular, General Thomas, head of the Department of War Economy and Armaments in the Army High Command, pointed out in a study that even if the military operations were successful, the value of Barbarossa to the war economy would be dependent on many risky factors and in any case would turn out to be much less than had been hoped.[193] The whole plan of attack was based on numerous uncertain assumptions, and overestimated the German capacity as much as it underestimated the strength of the Soviet Union. The gambler was chancing his last card. Everything depended on a quick victory in the manner of the previous *Blitzkrieg*. If the Soviet Union could not be conquered in a rapid campaign, if it could offer resistance until the British and Americans had mobilised their war potential, then Germany was lost. This fact was recognised by a general from the narrow circle of officers initiated into Operation Barbarossa, who asked the defeatist question: 'Can't you now see clearly that the war is lost?'[194] Indeed, even Hitler himself said, after an anxious discussion with some of his assistants on 29 May 1941: 'Barbarossa is also a risk, like everything else; if it fails, then in any case all is lost.'[195] His letter to Mussolini on 21 June 1941 is completely credible: in it he asserted that the decision to attack the Soviet Union had been the hardest of his life.[196] When the Germans crossed the border into the east the feeling often came over them – from the Führer down to the common soldier – that they were thrusting open a door into the unknown, behind which Stalin had wicked surprises in store for them, and that in the end doom might be lurking in the endless wastes beyond.

The War Against Europe

On both sides the stage was set for war. The nature of the German forward troop movements and advance is well known, but even today there are many unanswered questions about the Soviet deployment. Soviet figures about these dispositions and about the first weeks of the war are obviously so inaccurate as to prevent any deductions as to operational intentions and strategic and political goals. This leads one to assume that there is more to this than the familiar Soviet secretiveness or the widespread inclination of nations and armies to dwell on their victories rather than on their defeats. Certainly, it cannot be denied that facts which are of fundamental importance for a complete assessment of Soviet actions have been covered up. Recently, however, the Soviet Union has provided some clues which, together with German documents, make possible a reconstruction of at least the main features of the deployment of the Red Army.

It has already been mentioned (page 80f) that during the months following the end of the campaign in France the German military build-up in the east proceeded fairly slowly, but even later the troops there received only moderate reinforcements, possibly in order to conceal any intended moves as long as possible from the enemy. On 6 April 1941 – that is, at the beginning of the Balkan Campaign – there were altogether forty-seven divisions, of which only three were tank divisions, opposing the Red Army. These forces would have been much too weak for an offensive.[197] The actual attack forces – motorised and tank units – were only brought up at the end of May – from Germany, from the west or from the Balkans. On the other side, the Soviets had been continually strengthening their forces in the future arena of operations, so that their deployment cannot be considered a response to German troop concentrations.[198]

It is possible, however, that a short time before Operation Barbarossa was launched information about German plans may have filtered through and made the Kremlin hasten its preparations. In any case, the

Soviet deployment, now becoming more and more evident, was a source of concern for General Halder, Chief of the German General Staff, who was afraid of a preventive strike by the future enemy. The general wrote in his diary on 7 April 1941:

> If we ignore the current Soviet protestations that they want peace and won't themselves start an attack, then the present deployment of their forces must make us pause for thought and admit that this deployment is very well suited for a switch over into an attack, which would be most uncomfortable for us. . .[199]

This, however, is only conjecture based on the available information at the time.

It is worth noting that on 10 April a council of war under Timoschenko declared a state of emergency for Soviet fighting forces, even though at this time the Soviet Union could not feel itself directly threatened, since a considerable part of the German army, and especially the attack units, was tied down in the Balkans. According to all the evidence it is improbable that the Soviets intended to attack the Germans in the back during the Balkans campaign. This state of emergency was more likely to have been a demonstration to encourage the resistance of the Yugoslavs and the Greeks, and at the same time a test of the operational readiness of the troops. Any faults brought to light by this rehearsal could have given Stalin reason to start making greater efforts to gain time.

With Soviet preparations for war being pushed forward energetically according to the military doctrine (see page 70) of throwing back the aggressor and then destroying him on his own territory, the main question was to decide where the main body of the Red Army should await the German offensive. There were various opinions on this. Marshal Schaposchnikov, a veteran of the czar's General Staff and at that time certainly the most able strategist on the Soviet side, recommended that the main fighting forces should be drawn up within the old state boundary of 1938, leaving only covering troops in the newly-won western regions. But the general did not get his way – fortunately for the Germans, who would have been prevented from annihilating powerful Soviet units near the border if this plan had been adopted. When the proposal was made to transfer stores and supply bases for the troops on the western borders to behind the Dnepr, Marshal Kulik, a party favourite, abused the proposer and called him a defeatist:[200] so much caution seemed unnecessary, if not harmful. Instead it was decided to concentrate assault units in the western regions, a move which fitted in with German intentions and made no small contribution to the catastrophes of the first phase of the war.

In accordance with this basic plan, which emphasised attack, the defences on the old state border – usually called the 'Stalin Line' by the Germans – were partially disarmed and neglected, indeed at times they were said to be used by local farmers to store vegetables.[201] The weapons dismantled from there were built into fortifications constructed near the new western border. This confirms that Moscow did not expect any fairly deep incursions into the front, but was confident of being able to repulse any attack by the German army quite close to the border.

Further indications of the Soviet plan of action are given by the great concentrations of motorised and tank units in and behind the front lines, which protruded so as to form a bulge[202] around Bialystok and Lemberg[203]. About this General Halder correctly commented at a later hearing in Nuremberg: 'No troops deployed for defence would be concentrated in such numbers in an area projecting into the enemy'.[204] This has since been confirmed from Soviet sources. Marshal Schukov reported that the decision to concentrate troops in the Bialystok area had already been made in 1940,[205] and on this decisive point Major-General Grigorenko spoke quite frankly:

> More than half the troops of our Western Special Military Region were in the area round Bialystok and to the west of that, that is, in an area which projected into enemy territory. There could only be one reason for such a distribution, namely, that these troops were intended for a surprise offensive. In the event of an enemy attack these troops would already be half encircled. The enemy would only need to deal a few short blows at the base of our wedge and the encirclement would be complete.[206]

Here the intention to attack is portrayed without any shadow of a doubt; the Soviet failure was due to their belief that their own counter-attack would prevent the Germans from achieving such an encirclement. Regarding the bulge in the front around Lemberg there is evidence of even greater authority. Marshal Bagramian, who at the outbreak of war was a colonel and in charge of operations in the Kiev Special Military Region and therefore familiar with the situation, wrote about it as follows:

> The area protruding towards the west, including such a large town as Lvov, was considered to be a favourite deployment area in case we had to change over to a large-scale attack. It was not by chance that we had concentrated there two of our biggest and most battle-trained mechanised corps, the Fourth and the Eighth.[207]

What the author reports about a discussion with the newly appointed Commander-in-Chief of the Military Region, General Kirponos, in

106

which he himself took part – along with the Chief of Staff, General Pur-kaiev, and the high-ranking Commissar Waschugin – is also revealing. At this meeting the commissar emphatically supported the standpoint of the political leadership:

> It is not proper for us to be talking about defence. If our opponent forces war on us, our army will attack as no others have. We will crush the enemy there, on the very spot from which he has come.[208]

The military leadership was more aware of the difficulties. It is worth noting that Waschugin acted here not only on behalf of his superiors, but was himself deeply convinced of the correctness of his point of view. As a result of the impression made on him by the heavy reverses during the first weeks of the war he subsequently committed suicide.[209]

The staff of the Kiev Special Military Region was very well informed of German preparations. The head of intelligence, Colonel Bondarev, had received reports early in spring

> ... that the enemy is constructing a number of emergency landing grounds and branch railways, and that numerous unmetalled roads run straight to our border. In April large troop movements were begun which could perhaps have been a manoeuvre. Every manoeuvre and every exercise should have an end, but the advance of fascist troops up to the border never ceased. In the area bordering on the Ukraine up to two hundred trains arrived daily with troops and war materials.

At the beginning of June reliable news had come in that the Germans

> ... had requisitioned all military and other hospitals and sent their medical personnel there. Germans had been put in charge of all the main railway depots. All German military trains to the border were being accompanied by strong guards. On the territory of occupied Poland a state of war had been declared.

They had just learnt

> ... that the Fascists are everywhere replacing their border troops by regular army troops. Close to the border they are concentrating a vast number of requisitioned farm vehicles.

The Commander-in-Chief of the Air Force, General Ptuchin, 'pointed out to the council of war that there were frequent violations of the air space near our borders by German aircraft'. All this caused the Com-mander in Chief of the Military Region to make this statement:

One thing is clear: the situation is alarming. The fascists are making serious preparations aimed at us, either a great provocation in the manner of their allies, the Japanese Samurais, or . . .[210]

Kirponos's opinion was definite: it was war. Thus, from a most competent source, the myth of the 'malicious fascist attack on the unsuspecting Soviet Union' is exposed for what it is – a fiction created for the purposes of psychological warfare.

As a counter-measure, Kirponos ordered small forces of troops to occupy the prepared positions at the perimeter, so as to support the garrisons of the fortified areas and offer better cover for the deployment of further forces. The general had previously been ordered by a higher authority to hold all the units in the hinterland of the Military Region, which formed his second echelon, in readiness for an advance directly to the border.[211] It is worth mentioning that on the next day, under orders from the Moscow General Staff, the order to occupy the forward area had to be cancelled, since 'such measures could cause the fascists to provoke an armed conflict'.[212] But when it became more and more evident that a German attack was imminent the High Command gave, on 15 June, an order that all five infantry units should begin to transfer towards the border, in accordance with previous plans[213]. The lively and fairly detailed accounts of Marshal Bagramian likewise confirm Soviet intentions, which were to avoid any semblance of a provocation but to answer a German attack with a crushing counter-attack. In all this it can be assumed that the Soviet advance in the last weeks before the German invasion was not made because of a plan to take the initiative at that time – this was reserved, if necessary, for a later date. It is much more likely that in this case it was a reaction to information obtained about German troop movements.

Apart from the bulge-shaped front round Lemberg and before the ultimatum to Rumania – in May and June of 1940 – there had been strong concentrations of Red Army assault troops in the western Ukraine; these then moved into north Bukovina and Bessarabia and, in their new positions at the mouths of the Pruth and the Danube, caused some disquiet amongst the Germans. Here, at the gateway to the Balkans, German and Soviet interests had their earliest and most explicit clashes. The Soviet leaders wanted to push forward to the straits, but Stalin rightly assumed that for military and economic reasons Hitler would have to try to get hold of the Ukraine, the Donets Basin and the Caucasian oilfields.[214] The troops in these areas were therefore quickly put on a war footing and given preferential treatment in the allocation of new weapons and equipment. Behind the forces deployed around Lemberg and on the Pruth there were also battle-ready reserves in the area round Shitomir and Kiev, which could be diverted as required in one direction or another.[215] It was here that the Red Army offered the most stubborn resistance, although the main German thrust in the Ukraine came neither from Rumania nor from west Galicia via Lemberg, but from the area south-west of Lublin against Kiev. The central sector, with its bulging front, has already been mentioned. The forces concentrated there were definitely deployed for offensive purposes; how powerful they were was only completely revealed in the battles of Bialystok and Minsk, where enormous numbers of prisoners were taken, and quantities of artillery and tanks were captured or destroyed. In the Baltic area, opposing the German Northern Army Group, the preparations were not so far advanced: the troops had not opened out as much towards the border and there were fewer assault units – only four tank and two mechanised divisions. On the other hand, the Middle Army Group was faced with far stronger assault units under General Pavlov: twenty-four artillery, six mechanised, and two cavalry divisions. South of the Pripet Marshes – on an admittedly longer front – forty-five artillery, twenty tank, ten mechanised and five cavalry divisions were deployed.[216] These numbers refer only to the border defence areas, but not to those units to the east of these, which were already available or being made ready for action.

The main points in the assessment of Soviet dispositions made by Field Marshal von Manstein are still valid today:

> One will be nearest to the truth if one calls the Russian deployment a deployment for all eventualities. On 22 June 1941 the Soviet forces were certainly drawn up in such depth that, in view of their formation at the time, they could only be ready to carry out a defensive action. But the picture could have changed within a very short space of time. The Red Army could have opened up its ranks . . . in such a manner as to make it capable of advancing for an attack. Actually the Soviet deployment – even though up to 22 June it might have kept the form of a defensive deployment – represented a latent threat.[217]

Admittedly this applies primarily to the northern section, where Manstein had been sent at the beginning of the campaign. Further to the south Soviet preparations were already more advanced; but in any case, the picture as drawn by the field marshal accords with the well-known Soviet intention of first repulsing the German attack, then switching to a large-scale offensive. This is not contradicted by the fact that fortifications were built at various sections of the border. These could have been intended as a support for the troops in the initial defensive struggles, or as protection for sections where it was initially impossible or undesirable to go onto the attack. Throughout all the Soviet Union strategic reserves were established to supply the war operations. In

August more than 390 large units were identified before the German Army Groups, and there were very many more.[218]

There are further indications of the Red Army's offensive intentions. Of particular interest is 'Instruction No. 3', which the Soviet High Command issued on the evening of 22 June. This anticipated the Red Army 'going over to counter-attack, with the task of shattering the enemy at the most important sections of the front and pressing forward into his territory'.[219] In a similar vein, the south-west front commanded by General Kirponos received the order

> . . . to make permanently safe the state border with Hungary; to encircle and destroy the attacking enemy groups on the Vladimir-Volynski-Kryshopol front by concentric thrusts in the general direction of Lublin, and by the evening of 24 June to take control of the Lublin area, using for this forces of the Fifth and Sixth Army, at least five mechanised units and all the available front-line air power . . .[220]

Of course it was impossible to carry out these orders. They were not reactions to the realities of the situation but, without regard to the facts, merely reflected the familiar war dogma. The fact that numerous airfields were constructed fairly close to the border,[221] which would have been completely senseless for defence purposes, gives yet more evidence of the Soviet desire to invade Germany, with or without a German attack.[222] Captured documents and statements from prisoners fill in the picture. In Soviet military staff quarters maps of areas far beyond the Demarcation Line were found. This suggests that, for example, the Soviet motorised unit number twenty had been allocated a specific sector for attack, which extended over the Bug and far beyond the Weichsel, south of Warsaw, and into the west.[223] Such documents furnish clues as to the Soviet schedule. A captured document gave details of Soviet plans for attack, which must be completed by the late summer or autumn.[224] This date was often confirmed by officers who had been taken prisoner, amongst them General Vlassov.[225] All this certainly does not prove that the Red Army would have actually taken the initiative at this juncture, but the potential for attack was required.

No documents are available about the plans for such an invasion, but the deployment, even though not yet completed, supports some assumptions about Soviet operational possibilities and intentions. In the south, where the greatest progress had been made with the preparations, the first aim was certainly to take possession of the Rumanian oilfields, which were indispensable to the German conduct of the war. If these operations proceeded smoothly, Bulgaria was to be the next goal, which would leave the Red Army standing right in front of the Straits. Yet it would also be possible, through an insurrection in

Yugoslavia, to press forward to the Adriatic and so take a tight grip on the Germans with a pincer movement from the south-east. The bulging front round Lemberg offered various operational possibilities. An attempt could be made to penetrate forward through the Carpathian passes into the Hungarian lowland plain, which the Soviets had wanted to do in the First World War. Another alternative would have been an attack through West Galicia aimed at the industrial area of Upper Silesia, but the order to General Kirponos, already mentioned (page 108), is more indicative of an intended thrust to the north-west where, after surrounding and destroying the German army units attacking in the area around and to the south of Lublin, the way over the Weichsel could be cleared. Then, by co-operating with the mechanised columns pressing forward from the bulge in the front at Bialystok, a large-scale encircling operation in central Poland would be possible. In the framework of such a plan, the forces in the Baltic area would have had the task of advancing along the Baltic and so covering the northern flank. All this is speculation, but what Molotov had said in the air raid shelter gives it a certain credibility. Possibly these plans formed the basis for the Soviet offensives in the years 1944–45. Whatever the details may have been, they were never carried out at the time, and it is very doubtful if the documents still in existence will ever become available for research.

On the other hand another conundrum of the Second World War can very probably be solved: why did Stalin delay so long in warning his forces, and thus enable the Germans to inflict a number of tactical surprises with dire consequences for Red Army units? The Soviet dictator has been severely criticised for this delay and accused of being credulous, gullible or obstinate. However, considering the assumptions he had to make at the time his reticence was in fact both clever and responsible. There is no reason to doubt the account given later by Schukov, based on his own experiences of those events,[226] although admittedly he does not go into their political background. The ever more frequent reports of an imminent German attack were received by Stalin with great mistrust, and he was concerned neither to provoke the Germans nor to let himself be provoked by them. In this, as already mentioned (see pages 97ff) he had two main objects: to create the myth of an unprovoked attack and, for military reasons, to delay the coming conflict as long as possible. If he was misled into hitting out too soon, then the myth would be exposed and he would have to put an army not yet completely ready for war into action; and the same disadvantages threatened if he openly challenged the Germans. In the background there were, however, other considerations. It has been emphasised many times that Stalin regarded the British, and later the Americans, as his real enemies. Hitler had driven them from the continent for him, and now Stalin was beginning his campaign to overwhelm them. Was it not possible that Hitler – who was now to be liquidated – and the British and Americans – who were to be presented with a *fait accompli* – would see through his great plan and frustrate it? The prospect of German agreement with the British had always frightened Soviet foreign policy-makers, and moreover it was a tenet of communist logic that 'imperialist groups' then hostile to each other would join in conspiracy against the 'Fatherland of all Workers'. Rudolf Hess's mysterious flight to Scotland caused considerable nervousness in Moscow and Stalin feared a secret arrangement by which the Germans might become a tool of the British and Americans against the Soviet Union. Such fears had no firm basis, but the suspicious dictator believed that the Germans or the British hoped to provoke him into taking hasty action before the time was ripe.

In line with this, he forbade until the last minute any measure which might offer a pretext for the unleashing of an armed conflict.

> The People's Commissars for Defence, the General Staff and all commanders of the Border Defence Regions were told that they were personally responsible for the possible consequences of any careless actions by our troops. Unless we had Stalin's personal permission, we were strictly forbidden to transfer troops to the front line according to the plan for cover.[227]

The text of the alarm order, finally issued on 22 June 1941 at 0030 hours, is just as cautious:

> It is the duty of troops not to allow themselves to be misled by any provocative act which might cause complications. At the same time the troops of Defence Districts Leningrad, Baltic, Western, Kiev and Odessa have to be in a state of full alert to oppose a possible surprise blow by the German or their allies.[228]

When the German army began the attack three hours later this order had in many cases still not reached the forward units of the Red Army.

This enabled the Germans to gain a tactical advantage which made an essential contribution to their great initial successes. In particular, they succeeded in destroying a considerable number of Soviet aircraft on the ground, thus gaining mastery of the air in the area of operations. While this was happening the tanks thrust deep wedges into Red Army lines, whose deployment, though well under way, had not yet been completed, so that terrible confusion often ensued. Many units defended themselves literally to the last man; others surrendered after a short struggle. The biggest successes were achieved by the Central Army Group, which succeeded in surrounding Soviet assault units massed in and behind the bulge in the front at Bialystok and rapidly destroying them. The dream of an easy victory, of smashing the aggressor on his own territory and following up with a triumphant campaign in Europe vanished into nothing within a few days.

On the German side, illusions began to flourish. Even a very sober observer like General Halder wrote in his diary on 3 July 1941:

> It is not an overstatement if I say that the campaign against Russia was won in fourteen days. Of course, it isn't finished yet.[229]

Hitler, too, believed at the time that victory was already won, and indulged in fantastic plans for the future. But gradually it became clear that the Soviet Union was anything but a 'Colossus with feet of clay'. In spite of enormous losses, this vast empire could keep hurling new masses of men and material at the invader, and soon increasing numbers of the new types of tanks and the dreaded rocket-launchers appeared on the battlefields. The fourteen-day victory developed into a war lasting at least four years, fought with the greatest bitterness on both sides, and the dramatic victories of the first weeks turned out to be the beginning of the end for the Third Reich.

At first, however, the German army reaped the benefit of the incomplete state of Soviet war preparations – which had been one of the reasons why Stalin had initially wanted to avoid any open confrontation with Germany. And this was why he delayed ordering his forces to full alert for so long – not through thoughtlessness or gullibility, but quite the opposite – through an excess of caution. When Molotov had handed Stalin's summons to the Germans in Berlin and so provoked them the Soviet dictator was still convinced that his forces would be ready for war before the date of any possible attack by the German Army. But when this attack loomed the Red Army was not ready, in spite of enormous exertions. This was not mere chance. It was due – at least in part – to a structural pecularity of the Soviet system at the time: the yawning gulf between planning and reality, ideology and actuality. What Gustav Hilger had observed in the year 1932, on a journey made to study the politics and economics of the country, still applied in 1941: the juxtaposition of enormous ambition, modern techniques and equipment, and often astonishing achievements on the one hand, with primitive methods of working, negligence and other faults on the other hand.[230]

This was also true in the military sphere, but here, in spite of mighty

113

efforts and a brutal drive to achieve efficiency, reality was far too slow to catch up with the ambitious plans. When the German army began its attack not only was Soviet troop deployment incomplete, but also the whole of the Red Army was essentially unprepared. The Officers' Corps were still suffering from the purges of 1937–38. The tank forces were in the middle of a reorganisation, and re-equipping with new models of armoured cars had only just begun. New types of weapons and equipment were in many cases available in considerable numbers, but the soldiers had first to be trained in their use. The greatest deficiencies were in anti-tank and anti-aircraft weapons, but there was also a shortage of towing vehicles for the artillery. The Soviet air force was numerically far superior to the Luftwaffe, but it consisted for the most part of older aircraft which could not match the enemy in speed, armament or equipment. There was often a shortage of the skilled labour required for servicing and maintaining complicated technical equipment and apparatus. Communications systems were also particularly inadequate. Owing to the great distances involved the laying of telephone cables often turned out to be an impossible task, and as there were few amateurs in the totalitarian state there was no reserve of personnel for wireless communications. Moreover, even trained wireless operators were often not familiar with coding procedures, a fact which considerably aided the wireless intelligence service of the enemy.[231] Finally, local conditions and facilities offered little to meet the demands of widespread operations by strong forces. Especially in what had been eastern Poland the railway and road network was completely inadequate, and by the time the war started major improvements were impossible, rendering the movement of troops and supplies much more difficult.

These faults were known to Soviet leaders and were a major cause for concern, particularly for specialist officers; but in spite of this there was never any thought of questioning the basic military dogma. The ideology of the 'easy victory' and of 'smashing the enemy on his own territory' had at that time no military instrument at its disposal capable of achieving these aims in the real world, but nevertheless training and deployment were firmly based on that ideology. Mention has already been made (page 72) of the disastrous consequences of the exclusive concentration on attack during training, and the corresponding neglect of defence and retreat. These errors were aggravated to some extent by the further ideological dogma that class differences made the capitalist and 'imperialist' armies inferior to the Red Army. This erroneous view caused a disastrous underestimation of the Wehrmacht and misled the Soviet leaders into making a deployment designed for an early counter-offensive, in spite of the deficiencies they knew to exist. The concentration of powerful forces in the western areas in accordance with this doctrine facilitated the German campaign very considerably. The strategy of Operation Barbarossa was aimed at achieving a tactical surprise, which in its turn would lead to the encirclement and annihilation of the enemy forces near to the German and Rumanian borders before the Soviets could withdraw into the depths of their own territory. Thanks to dispositions of the Red Army the first phase of this strategy was a great success. In particular, the forces round Bialystok were handed over to the German army for encirclement, as if the whole action was a training manoeuvre.

It has already been emphasised (page 45) how greatly Hitler had profited from the serious, indeed incomprehensible mistakes of his opponents in Poland, Norway and France; now these events were followed by Soviet errors in troop deployment with even more disastrous results. However, the Soviet Union had a far greater potential of resistance. If only because of its vast extent, the powerful empire could not simply be subjugated in a lightning campaign, and Stalin's ruthless energy made sure that all reserves within the depths of the country were mobilised. Indeed, during the course of this frightful struggle the Soviet Union extended itself and took a decisive step towards becoming a superpower. By contrast, Germany was effectively diminishing itself with every step in its exhausting campaign in the east.

A Small Triumph

The German attack on the Soviet Union and the great initial success of the campaign had important consequences at various levels. First of all it caused the world coalition which brought about the destruction of Hitler's Germany and which decisively influenced the fate of Europe, indeed of the world, with repercussions that extended far beyond the later breach between the Allies.

From the very first moment it was evident that the Western powers had not the slightest intention of using Hitler as a tool against the Soviet Union – as Stalin suspected and as Soviet propaganda repeatedly asserted and still asserts to this day. When Operation Barbarossa was launched there was an opportunity to do this, but of course the last thing in the world London wanted was an agreement with Hitler. On 15 June 1941 Churchill had sent this wire to Roosevelt:

> Should this new war break out we shall of course give all encouragement and any help we can spare to the Russians, following the principle that Hitler is the foe we have to beat. I do not expect any class-political reactions here, and trust a German–Russian conflict will not cause you any embarrassment.[232]

The British Prime Minister remarked about Stalin on the day before the German attack:

> He believed that Hitler was relying on obtaining the sympathy of capitalists and conservatives in Great Britain and the U.S.A. But Hitler is wrong; on the contrary, we must do all in our power to support Russia.

To the suggestion that for him, the arch anti-communist, this was somewhat hypocritical he replied:

> Not at all. I have only one purpose, the destruction of Hitler . . . If Hitler invaded Hell, I would make at least a favourable reference to the Devil in the House of Commons.[233]

116

Churchill also said in his broadcast on the evening of 22 June:

> Any man or state who fights on against Nazidom will have our aid . . . It follows therefore that we shall give whatever help we can to Russia and the Russian people . . . if Hitler imagines that this attack on Soviet Russia will cause the slightest divergence of aims or slackening of efforts in the great democracies who are resolved upon his doom, he is woefully mistaken.[234]

He then very aptly described Hitler's intention of first defeating the Soviet Union in order subsequently to turn all his strength against the West: 'The Russian danger is therefore our danger and the danger of the United States'.[235] President Roosevelt was of the same opinion and so the British and the Americans began without delay to initiate generous aid for Russia.

While diplomatic relations soon started in this connection, Stalin personally kept very quiet and left it to Churchill to take the initiative at the highest level. On 7 July the British premier sent a message praising the resistance of the Soviet army and promising every possible assistance. Three days later he got Sir Stafford Cripps to hand over to Stalin the draft of a joint Anglo–Soviet declaration. The text obliged the governments of both nations to support each other in every way; they would never negotiate an armistice or a separate peace without mutual consent.

But in spite of his difficult military position Stalin did not grab eagerly at the help so generously offered. Not till 19 July did the Soviet Ambassador Maiski hand over his answer to Churchill. The Soviet leader agreed to an active alliance between the Soviet Union and Great Britain in the fight against Germany, and made known his conviction that in the end the two states would overthrow the common enemy. He then pointed out

> . . . that the situation of the Soviet Union at the front remains tense. Soviet troops are still feeling the consequences of Hitler's unexpected breach of the non-aggression pact and the simultaneous surprise attack on the Soviet Union, both of which have given advantages to the Germans.[236]

This statement seems remarkable since in April Churchill had sent Stalin an urgent warning of Hitler's intentions.[237] Nonetheless, Stalin insisted firmly and with consistent logicality – or should one say with consistent obstinacy – on maintaining his carefully prepared myth of the malicious, treaty-breaking attack inflicted on the trusting Soviet Union. And Churchill seems not to have seen through this subterfuge.

Scarcely less revealing is the following paragraph from the same letter:

> It is easy to imagine how much better the position of the German troops would be if the Soviet Union had not stood up to their attack in the regions of Kischinev, Lemberg, Brest, Kaunas and Viborg, but instead in the regions of Odessa, Kamenez-Podolsk, Minsk and the surroundings of Leningrad.

Here Stalin was giving a hint that in spite of his present troubled situation he had no intention of giving up the gains from his pact with Hitler. The dictator then demanded the setting up of a second front against Germany, either in the west in the north of France, or in the Arctic north. He suggested in the latter case that the British should land a light Norwegian volunteer division in northern Norway to organise an uprising against the Germans. But there wasn't such a division, and Churchill wasn't in a position to establish one.

About this Churchill remarked:

> Russian pressure for a second front started right at the beginning of our correspondence. During all the rest of our relationship, this topic was never let to rest, with monotonous disregard, except in the far north, for physical facts.[238]

Subsequently the British premier sought to make clear to his new ally, giving very valid reasons, the utter impossibility of such an enterprise, but without any success. He was almost like a desperate teacher with a dull-witted pupil. Yet the really dull-witted person was not in Moscow at the time. If the interpretation of events made in this investigation is correct, then Stalin was very well aware that his demands could not be met. He made them in spite of that – or perhaps even because of that.

Undoubtedly Stalin hesitated so long with his answer, after recovering from the initial shock, in order to await further developments on the military front, to ponder quietly over the new situation and to plot the most expedient strategy with regard to those whom he regarded as his most important opponents, even though they had now become his allies.

Although by the middle of July it was quite certain that the original plan for a Soviet campaign in Europe had to be abandoned, there were distinct signs that the German advance was beginning to slow down. Admittedly there was no question of a stabilisation in the military situation, but, assisted by the vastness of the Russian territory and his reserves in men and materials, Stalin could hope that in the end he would overcome the danger. He might perhaps have thought, even then, that after overcoming the crisis he could resume his expansionist policy against the west and realise as many as possible of his original intentions. At the same time – even as he co-operated militarily in the anti-Hitler alliance – the psychological and political warfare on the Western powers was to be continued. As before, the myth of the treaty-breaking and malicious German attack served this purpose well, but now it was further developed by the appeal for a second front. As always, it was important that the psycho–strategical moves in the game were not recognised as such. It was probably for this reason that Stalin placed special stress on these very themes in his first letter to Churchill. He wanted to find out how the British premier would react, and by so doing test his political intelligence. The Soviet leader could be satisfied with his findings.

Stalin's cause was certainly furthered by the fact that although the initial German successes had thwarted his original plan of attack, they also served to conceal his intentions from the eyes of the world. This endowed the myth of the unprovoked attack with a credibility which it could scarcely have gained otherwise. While the German radio, to the accompaniment of Liszt's *Préludes*, trumpeted forth one special announcement after another about conquered towns and hitherto unheard of numbers of prisoners and booty – later even the towers of the Kremlin appeared in the binoculars of German reconnaissance troops – it must have seemed absolutely bizarre to think that in Moscow they might have planned to defeat this opponent on his own territory in one swift campaign. And while the mighty empire mobilised all its reserves to save its capital, it was equally strange to think that Stalin might once have hoped that at this time his tanks would have been approaching the Atlantic coast.

Yet Operation Barbarossa not only covered up Stalin's plans to perfection, but ensured the complete success of his intention to thrust on to Hitler the odium of the aggressor. The successful tactical surprise and the extensive advances of the German army seemed to prove incontrovertibly that the Germans had cunningly attacked an unsuspecting victim, and in view of the notorious ruthlessness of the Führer, any shadow of doubt concerning the veracity of that myth must have appeared ridiculous. It was further confirmed by the senseless and brutal occupation policy of plundering and enslavement which was carried out in the conquered eastern regions. Not only did this drive the tortured people in droves into the arms of the partisans, but it also provided important propaganda material for the Kremlin. The arrogance of the self-styled 'Germanic master-race' and the atrocities they committed aroused horror and indignation throughout the world and to some extent made people forget the ill-treatment the Soviets had themselves meted out in similar situation, as for example during the 'Soviet-isation' of the Baltic states. This was all cleverly exploited by well-organised agitation and so produced, especially amongst the British and Americans, a wave of sympathy and solidarity with the unfortunate Russian people. Public opinion everywhere demanded rapid and generous aid for the victims of fascist aggression.

The accompanying ideological music was once again re-orchestrated to tune in with all this. It has already been mentioned that since the end of the western campaign, and especially after the development of conflicts of interest in south-east Europe, Soviet propaganda had adopted an increasingly critical attitude towards Germany; but at the same time the Western 'imperialists' had also been subjected to attacks of the greatest animosity. After the outbreak of the war in the east, however, Moscow once again conjured up the solidarity of all democracies against the fascist enemies of society – as if there had never been a pact with Hitler and as if Molotov had never declared that the war to save democracy from fascism was nonsensical and criminal (see page 55). Regardless of these facts, the propaganda was very successful.

Moreover, in his appeal for resistance against the German intruders Stalin did not lay emphasis on Marxist–Leninist ideology but on patriotic love of the fatherland. He was certainly convinced, first and foremost, that this would have a greater influence on his own people; but it is likely that he also hoped his propaganda would find sympathy in the Western democracies. He was mainly concerned with inculcating his present capitalist partners with the idea that he had abandoned all thoughts of a world revolution. For a while Hitler and Ribbentrop also nourished the illusion that the Soviet system had been transformed into a kind of nationalist dictatorship,[239] and many people in Britain and America in particular fell prey to the idea that the Red Army's struggle in the 'Great War for the Fatherland' was only serving to free the Russian homeland from a barbaric occupation. For this reason, in 1943, Stalin dissolved – at least officially – the Communist International, whose underground activities had always aroused great mistrust abroad.

The appeal for a second front was a more complex matter. Basically, it implied that the new allies would have to establish a position of power on the continent which, after the joint victory over Germany, could only be at the expense of Soviet plans for expansion. In view of the heavy military defeats suffered by his forces at the beginning of the war, Stalin might have accepted such a development, but he had little interest in encouraging it, and he also knew very well that the Western powers were incapable of mounting such a large-scale offensive at the time. When he obstinately insisted on his demand in spite of this he was obviously pursuing other aims – in this case psychological and strategic aims. In the first place he wanted to show to his struggling people that he was doing all he could to provide them with relief, but at the same time he wanted to arouse and nourish mistrust of the Allies, who were so obviously leaving the heroic Soviet Union in the lurch. Possibly this continual discussion about the second front would also cause Hitler to hold stronger forces in readiness for action against the Western powers and so weaken his army in the east. But Stalin's strategy was directed mainly against the British and Americans. The demand for a second front was an excellent means of exerting moral pressure of a kind which struck a very resonant chord in the British mentality.

> Month after month in the European theatre of war, the Allies had to be satisfied with the role of spectator, whilst the Russian armies had to sustain the whole impact of Hitler's enormous war machine. As a result of this, the Allied statesmen began to get – quite unavoidably, I fear – a deeply-rooted feeling of guilt and inadequacy.[240]

Thus remarks George F. Kennan. It is possible that the thoughts of the Soviet leader ranged far beyond this, that he was hoping his continual importunate demand would mislead the British and Americans into making a premature landing in western Europe, where they might suffer a defeat which would eliminate them for some time from a position of power on the continent.

Along with others, Churchill felt very keenly how the inability to offer military support to the embattled Soviet people increasingly agonised and worried the British people. The premier had to explain to them why there was no question of a second front and why Britain would be unable to undertake anything more than the shipment of all kinds of supplies – for some time to come. This led to Mrs Churchill taking over the presidency of a 'Help for Russia' campaign to collect donations for medicines and medical equipment which were shipped to Russia. This action was given a warm-hearted reception everywhere; even captains of industry donated considerable sums.[241] But above all the moral pressure exerted was ideal for strengthening the demand for the greatest possible deliveries of military and economic aid, which was much more important to Stalin than the establishment of any 'imperialist' forces on the continent.

These demands assumed such proportions and were often made in such a manner that Churchill nearly lost his patience. On 28 October 1941, in a letter to Sir Stafford Cripps, he expresses his displeasure in unmistakable terms. The Soviets

> . . . certainly have no right to reproach us. They brought their own fate upon themselves when, by their pact with Ribbentrop, they let Hitler

loose on Poland and so started the war. They cut themselves off from an effective second front when they let the French army be destroyed. If prior to June 22nd they had consulted with us beforehand, many arrangements could have been made to bring earlier the great help we are now sending them in munitions . . . We were left alone for a whole year, while every communist in England, under orders from Moscow, did his best to hamper our war effort . . . That a government with this record should accuse us of trying to make conquests in Africa or gain advantages in Persia at their expense or being willing to 'fight to the last Russian soldier' leaves me quite cold. If they harbour suspicions of us, it is only because of the guilt and self-reproach in their own hearts.[242]

This criticism of the Soviet leaders is not lacking in pungency and candour, but it also shows how little the British premier recognised, in spite of his anti-communism, that from a political point of view the whole war was essentially a Soviet attack on the Western democracies, in which Germany and later Japan served only as military surrogates.

But the Soviets benefited from being hardly less grossly underestimated by the Western powers than by Hitler. In the opinion of the British and Americans Soviet Russia – especially under Bolshevism – was much too inefficient to represent a real danger,[243] whereas, especially after the lightning campaigns of the first phase of the war, the military efficiency of Germany was very highly rated. The great initial successes of the Germany army in the east seemed to confirm this verdict on both counts. Many people in London and Washington believed that the Red Army couldn't resist the assault longer than a few weeks and it was even feared that the Allied supplies wouldn't arrive in time or would end up in the hands of the Germans. It was therefore above all necessary to avoid a Soviet collapse, which would seriously damage the strategic position of the Western powers vis-à-vis Germany. The Allies fully understood that at the moment it was in their best interest to support the Soviet Union. At that time they were little concerned about future events. Even Churchill, who bluntly rejected Stalin's claims, especially to the Baltic states, was of the opinion that Moscow did not represent a serious danger. He considered it probable that at the end of the war

> . . . the United States and the British Empire, far from being exhausted, will represent the most heavily-armed bloc with the most powerful economy that the world has ever seen; and that the Soviet Union will need our support for reconstruction much more than we will need theirs.[244]

Nevertheless, there were irrational factors to be considered as well as this erroneous assessment of power politics. In the case of the Western powers, war propaganda and war emotions were concentrated to such an extent on Hitler's Germany that it would have been difficult to make a change of course plausible to the currently very irate public opinion. Even such an experienced politician as Churchill had a one-sided fixation on the destruction of Hitler's Germany; realistic statesmanship only thrives in an atmosphere of coolness and objectivity.

The leaders of the Western democracies failed to appreciate that – quite apart from the current war situation – they were in the same favourable position which Stalin had originally envisaged for himself. They could have exploited the advantages emanating from this situation against the two totalitarian powers by letting them wage a war of attrition against each other – exactly as the Soviet dictator had planned to do with the 'imperialist' powers. No changes of allegiance would have been necessary, only intervention – measured out in appropriate doses of assistance for the Soviet Union and acts of war against Germany. But London and Washington failed to exploit this favourable situation

> . . . which inevitably would have handed over to the Anglo-Saxon powers the role as arbiter in world affairs. It is also possible that the power struggle between the two totalitarian states would have brought about an end to their regimes.[245]

Moreover, soon after the conclusion of the Russo–Japanese Neutrality Pact, the tensions between Japan and the United States increased. In Tokyo a bitter struggle between the moderate and radical wings of the government had been going on for some time; the former consisted of the court, large sections of the upper aristocracy, influential economic circles and the fleet, whilst the latter was composed mainly of the military. The Prime Minister had to treat both groups with caution, but in the end the radicals gained the upper hand. The efforts of the moderates to avoid a war with the United States were unsuccessful, partly because the attitude of the U.S.A. – and also that of London – became more and more obdurate. When, under pressure from the army, the Konoye cabinet agreed to the military occupation of all Indo-China, the British and Americans announced in July 1941 drastic economic sanctions. Japanese funds in the U.S.A., England and various dominions were blocked. In addition, England, India and Burma cancelled their trading agreements with Tokyo, the Panama Canal and Singapore harbour were closed to Japanese ships, and the U.S.A. even induced the Central and South American states to stop all trading with Japan. This meant the loss of imports vital to the country's war economy, such as tin, rubber and oil. Such a blockade must have seemed unbearable, even to the moderates. The Konoye government resigned and was replaced by a war cabinet under General Tojo. Final negotiations met with failure. On 7 December there followed the surprise attack on Pearl Harbour.[246]

In a certain sense these radical economic measures, adopted mainly on the initiative of Washington, formed an antithesis to the summons which Molotov had given to the Germans the previous November.

> It was as if, at the end of July 1941, a time fuse had been set off, which – in view of the restrictions on Japanese oil supplies – would trigger off a decision fairly soon; in view of the Japanese mentality, this would not be to capitulate politically to the Americans, but to attack the U.S.A.[247]

In this way Roosevelt wanted to bring about America's direct entry into the war.

To what extent the new agreement with the Soviet Union encouraged Tokyo in its decisions is debatable. But at the time Japan had nothing to fear from this direction, especially since the Soviet forces were tied down in the conflict with Germany. In any case – just as Stalin had intended with the neutrality pact – the Japanese became involved in a war with the Western powers.

> The Russian Empire is not a country, which can be really conquered, at least not with the forces of the present European States . . . such a country can only be subjugated by its own weakness or the effects of internal dissension [and Napoleon Bonaparte's campaign of 1812] did not succeed because the enemy government remained firm, and the people remained loyal and resolute.

This was the verdict of Clausewitz,[248] as was well known in Moscow in 1941, where the Prussian military expert had a great reputation. What applied to Napoleon applied – as became more obvious month by month – also to Hitler. Although his armies were still pressing forward, the Russian colossus showed no sign of weakness or internal discord. Any serious opposition had been torn out by the roots in the great purges, and the people gathered together to defend the native soil of Russia behind the heirs of the czars. Although the Germans had occasionally been greeted as liberators, the hopes people had of them soon turned into disillusionment, indeed into bitter hatred.

So six months after Barbarossa Stalin could look to the future with confidence. The increasing tension between Japan and the British and Americans enabled him to throw fresh, well-trained troops into the battle for Moscow, where they inflicted the first heavy defeat on the Wehrmacht, which was exhausted by the long campaign and the rigours of the Soviet winter. The war might last a long time yet, and demand great sacrifices, but the Germans had not succeeded in subju-

124

gating the Soviet fatherland in a lightning campaign. When America at last joined the company of those fighting against Hitler's Germany the die was cast: the rest was only a matter of time.

Pearl Harbour was an especially great triumph for Stalin. At last the Soviets were freed from the danger of a war on two fronts; the British and Americans were now involved in one instead. In particular, their fleets suffered heavy losses in the Pacific, and strong forces, tied down in the Far East, were unavailable for action in Europe. In the war which Stalin conducted – militarily against Germany but politically against the Western powers – Japan too had become his tool, in a certain sense. He therefore found himself more and more in a position where as far as possible he had to put plans for expansion into practice; and while he was clamouring as loudly as possible for a second front, his real aim, as before, was to present the Western powers with a *fait accompli*.

Although Churchill didn't see through the Kremlin's game he soon began to get worried. He wrote on 21 October 1941 – well before Stalingrad – to his Foreign Minister, Anthony Eden:

> I must admit that first and foremost my thoughts are directed towards Europe. It would be an unthinkable misfortune if Russian barbarism were to swamp the cultural independence of the old European states . . . Though it is difficult to say such a thing today, I still hope that the European family of nations will act together in a European council.[249]

By the time of the meetings between Churchill, Roosevelt and Stalin in Teheran at the end of 1943, the military situation in the Soviet Union had improved considerably and accordingly their intentions came into ever greater prominence. Some days after this conference one of the American participants summarised what aims the policies of Stalin and Molotov might be pursuing in a memorandum:

> Germany is to be divided up and must remain so. The states of East, South-east and Central Europe may not form themselves into alliances or unions. France is to be robbed of its colonies and foreign strategic bases, and not allowed to maintain more than nominal armed forces. Poland and Italy retain approximately their present territories, but it is doubtful if they will be allowed to maintain armed forces in keeping with the size of these territories. As a result of this, the Soviet Union would be the only important political and military force on the European Continent. The rest of Europe would be condemned to military and political impotence.[250]

Unfortunately, neither President Roosevelt nor his most senior advisors took notice of these far-sighted warnings.

A more important document relating to the political situation was brought by Roosevelt's confidant Harry Hopkins to the Quebec Conference of 17–24 August 1943. It allegedly came from an 'assessment of a senior military officer of the United States'. There were no exact details of the source. In the text, dated 10 August 1943, was the following, as R.E. Sherwood reports:[251]

> After the war, Russia will occupy a dominant position in Europe. After Germany's collapse, there is no power in Europe which might oppose Russia's enormous military strength. Admittedly, Great Britain is in the process of establishing a position in the Mediterranean against Russia, which may be useful for the balance of power in Europe, but here too it is questionable if England can assert itself against Russia, unless it is supported from another quarter. The conclusions to be drawn from these thoughts are obvious. As Russia represents the decisive factor in the war, it must receive every possible support and every effort must be made to win its friendship. Since it will have dominance in Europe after the defeat of the Axis, the development and maintenance of friendly relations with Russia is all the more important. *Finally, the most important factor which the U.S.A. has to consider with regard to Russia is the conduct of the war in the Pacific.* If Russia unites with us against Japan, the war can be ended in a very short time and so with fewer losses of lives and material than if the reverse were the case. If Russia were to adopt a negative or unfriendly attitude regarding the war in the Pacific, then the difficulties would become enormous and the operations would end in failure.

Sherwood adds:

> This assessment was of such great importance, because it summarised the policies which governed the decisions at Teheran and later at Yalta.

The text of this memorandum reads almost as if it had been written by a Soviet undercover agent, but this impression may be wrong. In any case it indicated the success of the policy inaugurated by Stalin – guided by Lenin's ideas – and based on the Neutrality Pact of 13 April 1941. This policy was to incite America and Japan against each other and play the one off against the other so that the Soviet Union could gain the position of dominance in Europe.

Meanwhile, the further the Red Army moved into Germany and brought Hitler's end closer, the more pressing were the doubts about the usefulness of the anti-Hitler coalition. This became especially obvious in Poland and the Baltic. Ever since its re-establishment after the First World War, the Polish state had been a source of tension between the Western powers and the Soviet Union, and the annexation of its eastern part in 1939 had increased this tension. With the formation of the coalition after the German attack, the fate of Poland once more became a bone of contention, as the Russians had no intention of handing over their share of the booty from the Hitler–Stalin Pact. This led to a series of altercations between the Kremlin on the one side and England and the Polish government in exile on the other, until finally the revelation of the mass murder of Polish officers at Katyn led to the severing of diplomatic relations between Moscow and the Poles in London. When Soviet forces pressed forward to the Weichsel in 1944 this problem became acute. A development was now initiated which was to reach its tragic climax in the great Warsaw revolt.

Similar tensions arose in the Balkans, especially in Yugoslavia and Greece, where in the autumn of 1941 a communist partisan movement was organised to fight against the occupying forces, but also to eliminate the non-communist resistance groups and so pave the way for their own seizure of power. This ushered in a tangled skein of political confrontations and armed skirmishes, in which the Germans, the Italians, Tito's partisans, the Tschetniks of General Mihailovic and the Ustasches of the short-lived state of Croatia all took part – as well as the leaders of General Nedić's Serbian puppet government and, in the background, London, Washington and Moscow. The victor turned out to be Tito. He was not, however, satisfied with playing second fiddle to Moscow and finally chose the path of complete independence.

In Greece conflict centred on the communist-led Hellenic Freedom Front (E.A.M.) and Colonel Zerva's non-communist resistance group, which fought against the occupying powers and also against each other. Moscow, meanwhile, directed propaganda against the Greek army and navy, which were integrated into the British forces in the Middle East. When the Red Army approached the Balkans there was even a mutiny in the Greek Brigade in April 1944, which the British managed to suppress without bloodshed. After the withdrawal of the German army from Greece, the British had a hard struggle to prevent seizure of power by the E.A.M., but partisan units under General Markos continued their activities in the northern border regions till they lost their operational basis when Yugoslavia was cut out of the eastern bloc.

Full of deep tragedy, but also politically very revealing, was the fate of the Warsaw revolt in August and September of 1944. The Polish underground army, which was connected with the government in exile in London, had been preparing for this action for some time and started the fight as Soviet troops advanced rapidly towards the capital. A few days before Moscow radio had urged the people to revolt but when they actually began to do this the radio station was cloaked in silence, Soviet troops halted at the gates of the town, their rifles at their feet, and the

Soviet air force offered no support to the Poles. The Germans then quickly gathered together their forces and started a counter-attack. When Churchill appealed to the Kremlin to give help to the beleaguered Polish fighters Stalin not only turned down the request in a brusque manner, but also refused landing rights to British and American planes, which needed to land at Soviet-controlled airfields after dropping weapons and supplies to the Poles. Moreover, he condemned the revolt, which his own radio had vociferously advocated a short time before, as a ruthless and terrible adventure which had cost great sacrifices amongst the people. A joint request from Churchill and Roosevelt was then rejected in an even more brutal manner:

> Sooner or later, the truth about the group of criminals who have embarked on the Warsaw adventure in order to seize power will become known to everybody. These people have exploited the good faith of the inhabitants of Warsaw, throwing many almost unarmed people against the German guns, tanks and aircraft. A situation has arisen in which each new day serves not the Poles for the liberation of Warsaw, but the Hitlerites who are inhumanly shooting down the inhabitants of Warsaw.[252]

Only when the fate of the revolt was sealed did the Kremlin offer any assistance – in order to create the impression that they were doing something for the Poles. After a heroic resistance lasting two months the rebels had to capitulate, and when the Soviets moved into the completely devastated city they brought with them a very amenable puppet government.

Although the British Cabinet was indignant about Moscow's behaviour, irrespective of party loyalties, it was found impossible in the West to decide upon any drastic sanctions, such as stopping the delivery of supplies to the Soviet Union. At that time, and also later, Churchill vehemently criticised the Soviet Union for its part in the disaster, recognising that Moscow wanted the complete destruction of the noncommunist resistance movement in Poland. But looking back over his memoirs it would seem that the implications of that tragic happening had escaped him. In point of fact, these events in Warsaw cast a blinding light on the actual political character of the whole war – as a Soviet-inspired attack on the great democracies. The Germans had loyally carried out their role once again, this time in Warsaw. They could have cleared out of the city and left it to the Kremlin to sort things out with the Polish underground army in their own manner with the whole world to witness the results, which would perhaps have been an eye-opener for many people. Instead of this the Germans once again did Stalin's dirty work for him.

In Washington the political roots at the basis of the war were even less understood. It is true that the American Embassy in Moscow, where Avrell Harriman and George F. Kennan served, gave repeated warnings about Soviet intentions, but with little success. Roosevelt stuck to his conviction that by patience, goodwill gestures and honest intentions the mistrust of the Soviet leaders could be overcome and they could be converted into benevolent partners for the welfare of all mankind. In spite of all experiences to the contrary, he stuck to this belief till he died.[253] The intentions of the American president were incomparably nobler than those of Hitler and his accomplices, but his lack of political acumen had disastrous consequences. Later Kennan, who had first-hand experience of such matters, bitterly criticised the portentous errors made by the Allied political leaders at the time:

> By that I mean the inexcusable ignorance about the nature of Russian communism, about the history of its diplomacy . . . I mean by that F.D.R.'s well-known conviction that although Stalin was a rather difficult character, he was at bottom a man like everyone else; that the only reason why it had been difficult to get on with him in the past was because there was no one with the right personality, with enough imagination and trust to deal with him properly; that the arrogant conservatives in the Western capitals had always bluntly rejected him, and that his ideological prejudices would melt away and Russian co-operation with the West could easily be obtained, if only Stalin was exposed to the charm of a personality of F.D.R.'s calibre. There were no grounds at all for this assumption; it was so childish that it was really unworthy of a statesman of F.D.R.'s standing.[254]

No wonder the cunning and suspicious Stalin could not comprehend such an excess of political incompetence, and continually imagined secret traps and hidden capitalist ulterior motives, where in reality there was only abysmal ignorance, vanity and naivety.[255]

In such circumstances, the resolutions of the European Advisory Commission on the future of Germany are hardly surprising. The English were represented by Sir William Strang of the Foreign Office and the two other great powers by their ambassadors in London, Winant and Gusev. At the beginning of 1944 this commission worked out the plan for the zones of occupation in Germany, and this was later carried out. Whatever considerations the British and the Americans may have had at that time, they were apparently not disturbed by the knowledge that the Red Army was to be stationed so far into the west, as intended by this plan.[256] These momentous decisions were made long before Yalta. In the summer of 1945 Stalin was able to keep the Western powers to their word, just as he had done in 1940 with the Germans over Finland. And just as he had safeguarded the offensive bulges of Bialystok and Lemberg by the treaties with Hitler and Ribbentrop, in the same way he now reserved for himself the Thuringian bulge, which protruded like a fist into the central Rhine area. In both cases it is hard to decide which is more astonishing – the far-sightedness and purposefulness of Stalin, or the lack of these qualities in his opposite numbers. Since the German attack the Soviet Union had borne the real brunt of the war and so relieved the situation of the British and Americans; but its leaders had themselves provoked the attack and only engaged in the conflict for their own ends. Their actual aims and secret intentions have already been mentioned many times. On the basis of these the Soviet Union could hardly make any morally justifiable demands on the Western governments. But at first the Soviet Union had possessed scant means of exerting political pressure, and even these were basically psychological in nature. Together with the already mentioned psychological and strategic myths and tricks was the threat of making a separate peace – something Ambassador Maiski had hinted at in London shortly after the war started. Later Stalin actually tried to establish contact with Hitler through intermediaries with this threat in mind, but nothing came of his attempts.[257] After his experience with the Soviets since 1940 Hitler was no longer prepared to entertain any such proposal. Moreover, Stalin, whose intelligence service may have had informants inside the highest circles of the Nazi leadership,[258] considered that such attempts had only a slight prospect of success, and perhaps he wasn't even serious about them. But the Western powers might be impressed by this – they still felt concerned at the idea of a new version of the Hitler–Stalin Pact.

In any case, the British and Americans, who had not the slightest idea that they themselves were the real target of Stalin's war, completely scotched any possibility of a separate peace by insisting on an 'unconditional surrender' and by sending supplies to the Soviets which made a considerable contribution to their ultimate success. In particular, the 470,000 vehicles, delivered mainly by the United States, gave the Red Army a strategic and tactical mobility without which their wide-ranging offensives after 1943 would have been impossible.[259] To this extent the British and Americans had only themselves to blame if after the war ended they were frequently confronted with a *fait accompli*. Stalin also played the Japanese card repeatedly and with great skill. Although a substantial proportion of the Anglo-American forces was tied down in the Pacific, Stalin had no intention of weakening the fighting power of his forces in Europe, in spite of the fact that Churchill and especially Roosevelt repeatedly asked him to help them in the Far East by armed intervention.

130

Thus the Soviet position kept on improving as the end of the war approached. If one barrier against the Soviet Union's expansionist policy had been removed by the destruction of the Habsburg monarchy in the First World War, the second one was now removed by the destruction of Germany. If the British and Americans were not willing to abandon the entire continent of Europe to Soviet dominance, then they were obliged to set up their own barrier. Whereas Churchill became more and more aware of this fact, Washington initially turned a very short-sighted eye to these geo-strategical facts of life.

After Roosevelt's death on 12 April 1945 the presidency was taken over by Harry S. Truman, who was a capable politician but had first to familiarise himself with the tasks at hand. He certainly did not ignore Churchill's urgent warnings, even though at first he was faced with numerous difficulties. The war with Japan had not yet ended and, in spite of the hopeless situation, Tenno's soldiers continued to fight with the utmost bravery. The results of experiments with the atom bomb were not yet known, so Truman was at first confronted with the prospect of a long struggle with heavy losses. In these circumstances it seemed only logical to transfer a large proportion of U.S. forces from Europe to the remaining theatre of war. The British would ultimately not have been capable of resisting the pressure of the Russian colossus in Europe alone. Stalin's Japanese card seemed to be a winner until the atom bomb created a new situation. It brought about the speedy capitulation of the Japanese, and also had a moderating effect on Soviet intentions.

Without this new turn in events the Western powers would have been in a most difficult position – for military and also for internal political and psychological reasons. Soldiers and their relations were insisting on rapid demobilisation and public opinion was still focused on Hitler's Germany as the real enemy. Churchill had still not grasped (nor had the American leaders) that during the whole war the Soviet Union, allegedly an ally since June 22 1941, had ultimately been the most dangerous opponent. Even in the summer of 1945 many things were hanging by a thread. It is therefore easy to imagine the kind of situation that would have faced the Western democracies if the Soviet Union had launched a successful offensive in the years 1941 or 1942. While not detracting from the unequivocal condemnation of the crimes committed by Hitler or in his name, one might be permitted, in view of the above hypothesis, to say that Europe owes something to the losses of the German army. A further thrust forward by the Red Army was initially impossible, but the Kremlin could always hope to create a revolutionary situation in the West by exploiting post-war suffering, and in this way outmanoeuvre the British and Americans. There were, especially in the occupied zones of Germany, millions of refugees and displaced persons whom the Soviets intended to use to stir up insurrections. Some time elapsed before Washington decided to counter such plans with generous reconstruction aid, but it did mean that in Europe the Soviets achieved only partial success.

After the defeat of Germany Stalin set about harvesting the fruits of his policy in the Far East. In Teheran and Yalta he had already been allowed to lay claim to the Kuril Islands and South Sakhalin; in return he had promised to attack the Japanese within two to three months of the victory in Europe. In doing so he was disregarding the neutrality pact signed with Japan on 13 April 1941, and on 5 April 1945 the pact was formally cancelled by the Soviet Union. Japanese efforts to get Moscow to arrange a peace with Britain and the U.S.A. on their behalf yielded no results. On 6 August the first atom bomb was dropped on Hiroshima and by 10 August Japan was ready to capitulate. But only from 9 August – the date of the destruction of Nagasaki by the second atom bomb – did the Soviets declare that they were at war with Japan. It must remain open to question whether by doing this Moscow was fulfilling its obligations, or whether just wanting to ensure that it would get its spoils in good time. This behaviour rather gives the impression of body-snatching, but in any case it fits in with the principles of a rationally based policy: to gain a maximum of success with a minimum of effort and risk.

Not only was Japan now eliminated as a power on the continent of Asia, but Moscow's position there vis-à-vis the Western 'imperialists' had been decisively strengthened. After the victory of the Chinese communists in 1949 the grand plan of a Soviet-dominated continental bloc in the Far East seemed almost realised. The attack on South Korea in June 1950 was intended to herald the final episode, but the conquest of all Korea failed because of the resistance offered, especially by the Americans; and in the long run the Chinese leadership was not prepared to go on playing the role of mere vassal of the Soviet Union, which eventually brought about a breach between the two great communist powers.

Summary and Future Prospects

This book contrasts with current interpretations of the Second World War in that an attempt has been made to describe the central role played by the Soviet Union, and to show how the fundamental character of the conflict was of a Soviet attack on the capitalist world, and especially on the British and Americans. According to the concept developed by Lenin as early as December 1920 Germany and Japan were to be manoeuvred into a position of conflict with the Western 'imperialists'. It was expected that a 'second imperialist war' would result, which in its turn would initiate a radical upheaval of the capitalist system. This upheaval would lead to revolutions, as had occurred in the wake of the First World War with the Bolsheviks' seizure of power in Russia. Over and above this the Red Army would have a decisive influence during the final stage of the war.

During the twenties this plan might have had a rather defensive character owing to the overall weakness of the Soviet Union; but as the country became stronger during the thirties much more stress was given to its offensive aspects. There were also increases in the tensions between the 'revisionist' powers, Germany, Italy and Japan on one side, and the smug Western powers on the other – tensions which with appropriate initial priming could explode into war.

The pressure towards world revolution was combined with a military policy inherited from the time of the czars, which had as its geo-strategical goal – at least as long as Britain and America could not be attacked directly because of their mastery of the sea – dominance over a continental bloc stretching from Brittany to Kamchatka. In the west, a key position was occupied by the German empire which, after the elimination of the Habsburg monarchy, could either form the last barrier against Soviet expansion, or could become a tool for Russia to use against the Western powers. In accordance with this, ever since the Treaty of Rapallo Moscow had been trying to prevent an agreement between Germany and the victors of 1918.

This policy was continued after Hitler seized power in Germany, after

133

which the slogan of 'anti-fascist solidarity' was intended to widen the breach between Germany and the Western democracies. When it became more evident that Hitler didn't want to associate himself with any system of collective security, but instead was aiming at gaining mastery over the continent, the tension with Great Britain and France increased. Moscow used this situation, and German ambitions towards Poland, to bring on the outbreak of the Second World War by guaranteeing Hitler the cover he needed on his eastern flank. As a result of this arrangement – as Max Weber had once warned – Germany became dependent on the Soviet Union and thus could be used by Stalin as a tool against the Western 'imperialists'. The Soviet dictator wanted to prevent a German defeat by giving out his help in appropriate doses, but he also wanted to impede a Germany victory and so make the war drag on until both sides were exhausted and no longer able to resist the communist revolution and the Red Army.

At first all seemed to go well. When Poland was invaded the Germans were regarded as the callous aggressors, and it was they who shed Polish blood on the battlefield, while the Soviet Union was able to annex the eastern regions without risk or trouble and so gain a dominant position over the Baltic states. In Norway, too, the German army performed an important service for the Kremlin by preventing the British and French from establishing themselves in this important strategic position. Thus far Moscow could be well satisfied with the use it had made of Germany, but the campaign in France brought about a decisive change. The Western powers were defeated, the British driven from the continent – now only the German army stood between the Red Army and the Atlantic. If Germany could be subjugated Stalin would be master of the European continent and the British and Americans would be powerless to prevent it. For the time being Moscow could not anticipate getting much more use out of its tool. The Moor had served his purpose.

A phase of the war then began in which Soviet efforts were directed militarily against Germany but politically against the British and Americans. Ever since the end of the campaign in France the Soviets had been seeking to gain improved vantage points for an offensive in the west; they had also been further accelerating their arms production. However, the planned conquest of Germany needed careful political preparation. Molotov issued his challenge in November 1940 only when he knew for certain that the Germans couldn't come to any arrangement with the British. Hitler was now faced with two alternatives: either hand himself over completely to the Soviets, or offer resistance. If he chose the first option Moscow would have achieved a decisive success with neither risk nor effort; but if Hitler could be provoked into an attack then it was considered that in accordance with the prevailing military doctrine the Red Army could achieve an easy victory by a devastating counter-attack, devastate the Germans on their own territory and present the British and Americans with a *fait accompli* in Europe.

If the German army took the initiative and initiated hostilities there would be other advantages – especially in the creation of the psychologically and strategically valuable myth of the fascist aggressors breaking the treaty with Moscow and maliciously attacking the peace-loving Soviet Union. With the help of this myth Stalin hoped to motivate the Red Army and the whole Soviet people into making an extraordinary effort to repulse the invaders, but even more important was the influence it was expected to have on the British and Americans. To public opinion in these nations the Soviet Union could present itself as the latest victim of the insatiable German dictator's greed for conquest; it could also hide its own intentions and disguise the planned advance into Europe as retribution for Hitler's perfidious attack. At the same time it could set in motion a worldwide campaign of sympathy and solidarity with this anti-fascist crusade, thus exerting considerable pressure on the politicians in the Western democracies.

Although the unexpected initial success of the German army foiled the Kremlin's plans, it also gave greater credibility to that myth. The Western democracies let themselves be bamboozled almost to perfection, and even Churchill failed to grasp that the political core of the whole war represented nothing more nor less than an indirect Soviet attack on the British and American 'imperialists', in which Germany and later also to some extent Japan would simply play the role of military surrogate for the Soviet Union.

According to Stalin's plans Japan – a continual source of tension and trouble for the Soviet Union – was to be turned round and employed against the British and Americans. This goal was assisted by the neutrality treaty of 13 April 1941 by which Moscow was guaranteed the cover in the east that it needed for the war with Germany and at the same time gave similar assurances to Japan, thus freeing that country for an armed conflict with the British and Americans. Roosevelt's harsh policy towards Japan fell completely in line with Kremlin intentions and eventually led to the attack on Pearl Harbour – which signalled the outbreak of the 'imperialist war' in the Far East and gave evidence that the manipulative concept devised by Lenin and developed by Stalin had largely been realised. From then on a large proportion of U.S. forces would be tied down in the Far East and unavailable for action in Europe. In any event, the Kremlin could hope to oust the Japanese and Western 'imperialists' from the East Asian continent and establish its own predominance in this area.

By the end of 1941 Japan was putting pressure on the British and

Americans and the ultimate failure of the German *Blitzkrieg* was becoming obvious, so that Stalin could again start thinking of realising his original plans for Europe as widely as possible, in spite of the initial defeats suffered. For this it was imperative, as it always had been, that the British and Americans governments did not see through his intentions. But both nations were exclusively obsessed with the idea of destroying Hitler's Germany, which was considered to be the real opponent. In the post-war period nebulous speculations were indulged in concerning a world organisation – which eventually came into being with results that are well known. All these facts need to be appreciated if one is to understand how the British and the Americans, who at that time were not faced with any *faits accomplis*, had no second thoughts – even at the beginning of 1944 – about handing over to the Soviets a zone of occupation in Germany which protruded so far to the west. Churchill did begin to realise what was going on in Europe, but his attempts to open the eyes of the Americans were in vain. In the end he was faced with a *fait accompli*, as he explained at the end of the war in Europe:

> There would be little sense in punishing the Hitlerites for their crimes if law and justice did not rule and if totalitarian or police governments were to take the place of the German invaders. We seek nothing for ourselves. But we must make sure that those causes which we fought for find recognition at the peace table in facts as well as words, and above all we must labour to ensure that the world organisation which the United Nations are creating at San Francisco does not become an idle name, does not become a shield for the strong and a mockery for the weak.[260]

In this way the Soviet Union was able inflict a heavy defeat on the Western powers in the Second World War using purely political and strategic means. The Red Army never needed to cross swords with British or American forces: this was done for them by the Germans and the Japanese. Britain and America, indeed, shipped abundant supplies to the Soviet Union – far more than were needed to prevent a German victory in the east. Under the influence of the emotions engendered by the war against Hitler and the psycho–strategical tricks of Stalin – the myth of the unprovoked fascist attack and the continual demands for a second front – neither politicians nor public in the great democracies appreciated that the most dangerous enemy isn't necessarily the one directly embroiled in military conflict. Through this art of indirect, concealed and undramatic advances, which Stalin developed in masterly fashion, the cunning Georgian achieved his greatest success. The weakness of the Western powers was not due to a lack of the instruments of power, but to a deficiency in political intelligence.

But the Second World War was only a phase – though an important

136

one – in the realisation of Lenin's grand strategy to subjugate the capitalist or 'imperialist' nations – in other words, all those which had not yet undergone the process of Sovietisation. The 'worldwide anti-imperialist struggle' was continued and after England had ceased to be a great power Soviet efforts were concentrated on the U.S.A. – especially by mobilising the Third World against that nation – once again in accordance with the thoughts of Lenin. There are instances too numerous to mention of his strategy in operation – it is an example, indeed a model lesson in sophisticated power politics, and as such deserves speical consideration.

> He acts rationally and purposefully who sets his course of action according to the ends, the means needed for these ends, and any possible secondary effects produced, and whilst so doing, rationally balances off against each other both the means against the ends, the ends against the secondary effects, and finally the various possible ends against each other.

This classical definition by Max Weber[261] can be used as a starting point, and may also be considered as the basic principle of rational and purposeful action, which achieves maximum success with minimum expense and minimum risk. Although according to Weber[262] violence can indeed be considered as a specific means of political action – and the ultimate reason for it – such action must not be taken to be the only – nor in many cases the most expedient – means, as very often its use involves great expense and great risk. It can also result in failure, especially when the means gain the upper hand over the ends, or when there is uncertainty about the political situation which the use of force is intended to produce. Under certain circumstances, therefore, a military victory can lead to a political defeat; but it cannot, of course, be denied that a shortage of military power can decisively jeopardise a successful policy and often make it impossible to implement.

That violence can only be used as a means was explicitly emphasised by Clausewitz:

> War is an act of violence used to compel the opponent to carry out our will . . . Violence is therefore the means; to enforce our will on the enemy is the end we are seeking. In order to achieve this end, we must make the enemy defenceless and this is the correct conception of the real goal of warlike actions.[263]

However, if the purpose of war is to render the opponent (or the intended victim) defenceless and to break his will, there arises then the question as to whether this end cannot be achieved by means other than the use of force, and indeed perhaps with infinitely less effort and risk. Such means can be used to prepare, complete and support military action, possibly even to replace it. Bribery is an old and well-tried means: centuries ago the Persian kings used their 'golden archers' very successfully against the Greeks, and since then these methods have become considerably more involved. Sometimes it is possible to obtain at no cost the co-operation of persons because they are in sympathy with a given ideology. Attempts can made to employ a kind of *agent provocateur* and 'multipliers', a procedure which is especially suitable for influencing policies and public opinion in the democratic states. By using such peaceful techniques on the future opponent or victim, it is not only his will which may be influenced in the desired manner, but also the very roots of his motivation and political awareness, with all the various courses it might follow. In all this, semantic skill and the studied manipulation of language plays an important role. It must once again be emphasised that such methods can be used by totalitarian states against democratic states, but hardly ever is the reverse true, for totalitarianism allows no freedom of speech or public opinion, which might be manipulated from abroad. Foreign broadcasts are jammed and undesirable printed matter is confiscated at the border. The media are staffed by reliable supporters of the government who can only broadcast what their superiors allow and whose programmes are subject to rigorous monitoring. This enables the totalitarian states to enjoy a decisive psycho-strategical advantage – built into the framework of the state – which therefore cannot be compensated for by the democracies, and of course the dictators know how to make the best use of this advantage. This was well understood by Hitler and his entourage. His confidant at the time, 'Putzi' Hanfstaengl, once said:

> We will always be superior to the democracies in guiding their public opinion according to our wishes . . . Democracies cannot defend themselves against such attacks, that lies in the very nature of things, otherwise they would have to use authoritarian methods themselves; but dictatorships are protected against these weapons, so that they don't have to fear similar attacks.[264]

The various forms of the social use of tools make it possible considerably to reduce expense and risk, which in borderline cases can even be eliminated entirely. These different methods are most effective when neither the tool nor the object of manipulation can penetrate the actual connection or see through the hidden game being controlled from the background. Such blindness can stem from a lack of political intelligence, from emotional bias, or from a combination of both. That was how Hitler groped his way into Stalin's trap: with his sights set firmly on the conquest of Poland, he failed to grasp the Soviet dictator's ulterior motives. In the West, on the other hand, war emotions and war propaganda were so one-sidedly directed against Nazi Germany that for a very long period no one was able to form a sober, balanced judgement of the broad sweep of global politics. Churchill regarded the war as a personal duel with Hitler; Roosevelt was completely engrossed in his liberal masonic internationalism. Even after Yalta the U.S. President and his confidant Hopkins were in a euphoric mood and believed that a new day had dawned, '. . . the day which for some years we have longed for and about which we have spoken so much'.[265] M. Boveri rightly remarked that this was the language of a man dazzled by ideology.[266] Roosevelt was not at all conscious of what had really happened. But there were other misjudgements which also had dire consequences – in particular the gross under-estimation of the Soviet war potential. Moscow was also helped by the fact that the range of ideas of the leading American generals was narrow and military, while the top-ranking politicians hadn't enough vision to see beyond the defeat of Germany and Japan, and gave no thought to the geo-strategical consequences and implication of these events. Their field of view was so narrowly restricted to their immediate military opponents that they did not realise where their most dangerous political antagonist was operating from.

The above implies that anyone carrying out even the most sophisticated policy cannot create all the conditions for success, but is more or less dependent on the remaining actors falling in with his purpose. This applies especially to 'psycho-strategy', provided no compulsive measures are put into operation. Even the most strenuous efforts are in vain if the people concerned remain unimpressed, or even see through the hidden intentions. In such cases uncertainty and risk will not be eliminated: chance and luck will often play an important role. Nevertheless, within this framework political intelligence can achieve much. If it was once possible to use Hitler as a military tool when he was alive, then even today a dead Hitler serves as a psycho-strategical tool, helping to make credible in Germany or elsewhere an alleged fascist danger. This manipulation can admittedly only be successful on condition that the public have not become consciously aware of the fact that anti-fascism is nothing more or less than an instrument of pure power politics. In changing circumstances it is admittedly very important to adopt the means best suited to the prevailing conditions, and to exploit the emotional bias or lack of political intelligence displayed by allies or enemies; but nevertheless the decisive factor is the long-term objective, which must be pursued with unflinching consistency, irrespective of temporary successes or reverses, and which must have priority over everything else.

139

Postscript to the English Language Edition

Since the appearance of the first German edition of this book in April 1985, Victor Suvorov has published two articles of particular interest in the *Journal of the Royal United Services Institute for Defence Studies*.[267] Suvorov is a product of the Brezhnev era, a former member of the Soviet General Staff and one of the new generation of Soviet officers, but he now lives in the West.

The interpretation given here of the offensive character of the Soviet troop deployment early in 1941, and of Stalin's intention to 'liberate' Europe by a full-scale attack, is strikingly confirmed and supplemented by Suvorov's articles. In one respect, however, there is a considerable divergence. Suvorov is also of the opinion that Stalin had not originally planned to enter the war until 1942. For this purpose an attack force of hitherto unheard-of dimensions was to be created, with ten paratroop and twenty-nine mechanised units, each having 1,031 tanks. But Stalin was afraid that the war between Germany and Great Britain could in the meantime lose its impetus, or perhaps finish altogether. He therefore decided to bring forward the date of the attack. Once the Soviet armed forces in the Military Border Regions had been strengthened a massive deployment was begun in May 1941 in great secrecy. Under the guise of transfers to summer camps, preparations for manoeuvres or testing out the railway network, Soviet attack forces were pushed nearer and nearer to the border. By mid-June this deployment had progressed so far that it could no longer be put into reverse. Stalin had to attack now, irrespective of what Hitler did. Suvorov summarises his arguments as follows:

> Certain conclusions are incontrovertible. First, *the mobilised divisions could not have returned to the distant districts from whence they came*. Such a move again would have absorbed the entire resources of the railway network for many months and would have resulted in economic catastrophe. Secondly, *these gigantic forces could not have been left to spend the winter where they were hidden*. So many new divisions had been created and assembled in the frontal belt that many of them had

already had to spend the winter of 1940–41 in dug-outs. As early as 1940 there had been insufficient training centres and artillery and rifle ranges in the newly-acquired western frontier zone even for the existing divisions. Troops who cannot train rapidly lose the capacity to fight.

In every major human endeavour there exists a critical moment at which events reach a point of no return. This moment for the Soviet Union fell on 13 June 1941. After that day masses of Soviet troops were secretly but inexorably moving towards the German border. Once 13 June had passed the Soviet leadership could no longer turn these troops back or even halt them, for economic and military reasons. War became inevitable for the Soviet Union, irrespective of how Hitler might have acted. Finally, the composition and disposition of the forces in the frontier zone did not indicate that they were intended to remain there. Such features as the airborne corps in the first crust of the 'defences', artillery units in the forward locations, the dismantling of the Stalin line and the absence of any defence in depth or effort to construct one do not point to the intention of maintaining any permanent defensive position along the border. If all this is viewed in the context of the Zhukov doctrinal framework outlined earlier, then it becomes clear that the only credible military intention which Stalin could have had was to begin the war himself in the summer of 1941.[268]

Suvorov's picture coincides with that of Field Marshal von Manstein (see page 109) that on 22 June 1941 the Red Army could have made ready for attack in a very short time. It also fits in very well with the details given by Marshal Vassilevski (see page 71ff).

Suvorov has made a valuable contribution to the further clarification of the military preparations of the Soviet Union, but it does seem questionable whether the bringing forward of the deployment to 1941 and its enormous acceleration from May of that year was really due to the reasons Suvorov gives. More likely is the assumption that it was a reaction by the Soviets to real or intended German plans of attack which had in the meantime become known to them.

But more important than such detailed questions is an understanding of the deep-rooted political implications of the Second World War as a part of the Soviet long-term strategy for the subjugation and destruction of the non-communist world. The enormity of the crimes ordered by Hitler or committed in his name should not be used to divert attention from this fact. In many ways this book has been written more for the English-speaking than for the German reader. With the present edition it finds its way to the public for whom it was intended. I thank Mr Taylor for his indefatigable efforts in making this possible.

Ernst Topitsch, Graz, April 1987

Notes

1. H. Kummer, *Sozialverhalten der Primaten*, Berlin 1975, pp 152 ff. C. Vogel, 'Zum biologischen Selbstverständnis des Menschen' in *Naturwissenschaftliche Rundschau 30* (1970), reprinted in A. Altner (ed.), *Der Darwinismus*, Darmstadt 1981, pp 413 ff, especially pp 428 ff. F. de Waal, *Chimpanzee Politics*, London 1982.
2. E. Topitsch, 'Machtkampf und Humanität' in *Gottwerdung und Revolution*, Munich 1973, pp 135 ff, especially pp 150 ff.
3. G. Ritter, *Die Dämonie der Macht*, Munich 1948, p 89.
4. G. Gafencu, *Vorspiel der Krieg im Osten*, Zurich 1944, p 255.
5. G. K. Schukov, *Erinnerungen und gedanken*, Stuttgart 1969, p 226.
6. A. Hillgruber, *Der Zweite Weltkrieg 1939–1945*, third edition, Stuttgart 1983, p 59.
7. W. Hofer, *Die Entfesselung des Zweiten Weltkrieges*, fourth edition, Frankfurt 1964, pp 121, 132. Cf A. Hillgruber (note 6), p 19, and others.
8. J. W. Stalin, *Werke*, vol. 7, Berlin 1952, p 11.
9. A. Hillgruber, *Hitlers Strategie, Politik und Kriegführung 1940–41*, Frankfurt 1965, p 306, note 17.
10. J. Erickson, 'Kriegsvorbereitungen der Sowjetunion 1940/41' in A. Hillgruber (ed.), *Probleme des Zweiten Weltkrieges*, Cologne/Berlin 1967, pp 75 ff and quote on p 85.
11. G. Stökl, *Russische Geschichte*, Stuttgart 1962, p 318.
12. G. Gafencu (note 4), p 40.
13. H. Uebersberger, *Österreich zwischen Russland und Serbien*, Cologne/Graz 1958, p 2.
14. Ibid, p 3.
15. Ibid, pp 5 ff. G. Stökl (note 11), p 510. On Russian subversive activity directed against the Habsburg monarchy in the Metternich era see H. von Srbik, *Metternich*, vol. 1, Munich 1925, pp 569 ff. This also applies to the following paragraph.
16. On Danilevski's views about political aims and his influence in general see H. Uebersberger (note 13), pp 70 ff.
17. V. I. Lenin, *Werke*, vol. 26, Berlin 1964, p 178.
18. G. F. Kennan, *Sowjetische Aussenpolitik unter Lenin und Stalin*, Stuttgart 1961, pp 91 ff.
19. V. I. Lenin, *Werke*, vol. 31, Berlin 1964, p 434.
20. Ibid, p 437. Precisely in this sense Moscow declared during the Second World War 'that the U.S.S.R. has no sympathy for Germany's and Japan's imperialism, but is using it to crush the imperialism of England and America'. (Quoted from R. Cecil, *Hitlers Griff nach Russland*, Graz/Vienna/Cologne 1977, p 176).
21. Ibid, p 446.
22. Ibid, p 444.
23. G. F. Kennan (note 18), p 304.

24. V. I. Lenin (note 17), p 436.
24a. D. Shub, *Lenin – eine Biographie*, Wiesbaden 1958, pp 275 ff.
25. V. I. Lenin (note 17), p 442.
26. M. Weber, *Gesammelte politische Schriften*, second edition, Tübingen 1958, pp 109 ff (quote on p 120).
27. Ibid, p 124.
28. Ibid, p 121.
29. Ibid pp 152 ff (quote on p 157). H. von Srbik (note 15), p 624.
30. G. F. Kennan (note 18), p 300.
31. G. Hilger, *Wir und der Kreml*, second edition, Frankfurt/Berlin 1956, pp 185 ff, 259. General Ernst Köstring, *Der militärische Mittler zwischen dem Deutschen Reich und der Sowjetunion 1921-1941*, ed. H. Teske, Frankfurt.
32. G. Hilger (note 31), p 157.
33. On the finances of the NSDAP see J. Pool, *Hitlers Wegbereiter zur Macht*, Berne/Munich 1979.
34. F. Halder, *Hitler als Feldherr*, Munich 1949, p 22.
35. H. Rauschning, *Gespräche mit Hitler*, Zurich 1940, pp 15, 174.
36. Ibid, pp 123 ff.
37. G. Hilger (note 31), p 251.
38. For the attitude of the French bourgeoisie see for instance C. Bloch, *Die Dritte Französische Republik. Entwicklung und Kampf einer parlamentarischen Demokratie (1870-1940)*, Stuttgart 1972, especially pp 456 ff.
39. H. Pächter, *Weltmacht Russland*, Munich 1970, p 150.
40. A. Koestler, *The God that Failed. Six Studies in Communism*, London 1950.
41. G. F. Kennan (note 18), pp 424 ff.
42. W. S. Churchill, *Der Zweite Weltkrieg I/1*, Berne 1948, p 113.
43. Ibid, pp 142 ff. On the pacifist tendencies in the Labour Party at the time see also M. R. Gordon, *Conflict and Consensus in Labour's Foreign Policy*, Stanford, California 1969, pp 45 ff.
44. W. S. Churchill (note 42), p 117.
45. On these questions see W. J. Mommsen and L. Kettenacker (eds), *The Fascist Challenge and the Policy of Appeasement*, London 1983.
46. L. Kettenacker, *Die Diplomatie der Ohnmacht*. On the failure of the British government's peace strategy before the outbreak of war see W. Benz and H. Graml (eds), *Sommer 1939. Die Grossmächte und der Europäische Krieg*, Stuttgart 1979, pp 223 ff.
47. J. B. Doroselle, *La Décadence 1932–1939*, Paris 1979.
48. F. Hossbach, *Zwischen Wehrmacht und Hitler 1934–1938*, second edition, Göttingen 1965, pp 164 ff, also F. Halder (note 34), pp 19 ff.
49. L. Beck, *Studien*, Stuttgart 1955, p 63.
50. W. S. Churchill (note 42), p 398.
51. L. Kettenacker (note 46), pp 240 ff. A. Adamthwaite, 'France and the Coming of War' in Mommsen and Kettenacker (note 45), pp 246 ff, 251.
52. G. Niedhart, *Grossbritannien und die Sowjetunion 1934–1939*, Munich 1972, pp 148 ff. On the mistrust of the U.S.A. towards the Soviet Union, especially in the State Department and the diplomatic service, see F. Knipping, *Die amerikanische Russlandpolitik in der Zeit des Hitler-Stalin Paktes 1939–1941*, Tübingen 1973, pp 22 ff. From 1935 on right-wing circles suspected the existence of a communist-guided plot to undermine Roosevelt's administration; on the other hand Stalin's policy of the anti-fascist front gained new sympathisers in the years 1935–36, especially amongst liberals and intellectuals.
53. S. Allard, *Stalin und Hitler*, Berne/Munich 1974.
54. P. Schmidt, *Statist auf diplomatische Bühne*, Vienna 1950, p 464.
55. G. Hilger (note 31), p 285.

56. G. F. Kennan (note 18), p 336.
57. Ibid, p 360.
58. W. Hofer (note 7), pp 231 ff.
59. Ibid, pp 59 ff. G. Niedhart (note 52), pp 14 ff, 224.
60. K. D. Erdmann, *Die Zeit der Weltkriege*, Stuttgart 1976, p 488.
61. A. Hillgruber (note 6), p 18.
62. W. Hofer (note 7), p 135.
63. H. A. Jacobsen, *Fall Gelb. Der Kampf um den deutschen Operationsplan zur West-offensive*, Wiesbaden 1957.
64. W. Hofer (note 7), pp 150 ff.
65. F. Blaich, 'Wirtschaft und Rüstung in Deutschland 1933–1939' in Benz and Graml (note 46), pp 33 ff (quote on p 61).
66. Ph. W. Fabry, *Die Sowjetunion und das Dritte Reich*, Stuttgart 1971, pp 191 ff.
67. Ibid, pp 192 ff. In fact, after the beginning of Germany's surprise attack on Norway, the *Weserübung*, the Soviets increased their supplies since this operation was in their interests: see A. Seidl, *Die Beziehungen zwischen Deutschland und der Sowjetunion 1939–1941. Dokumente des Auswärtigen Amtes*, Tübingen 1949, pp 174 ff.
68. Hitler himself finally realised this, as can be seen from his description of events running up to the war in the east, dictated on 15 February 1945 to Martin Bormann: see A. Hillgruber (note 9), pp 360 ff, note 45.
69. A. Hillgruber (note 9), pp 45 ff.
70. A. Seidl (note 67), p 127.
71. A. Rossi, *Les communistes français pendant la drôle de guerre*, Paris 1951, p 57.
72. This information had been given by Colonel Oster to the Dutch military attaché Colonel Sas, who passed it on.
73. E. Bauer, *Histoire controversée de la deuxième guerre mondiale 1939–1945*, second edition, Monaco 1966, pp 88 ff.
74. H. J. Lorbeer, *Westmächte gegen die Sowjetunion 1939–1941*, Freiburg 1975.
75. R. van Overstraeten, *Albert I–Leopold III. Vingt ans de politique militaire belge 1920–1940*, Paris/Brussels, pp 520 ff. E. Topitsch, 'Die belgische Neutralitätspolitik 1936–1940 und die Katastrophe von Sedan' in *Geschichte und Gegenwart*, no. 1 (1982), pp 125 ff.
76. W. S. Churchill (note 42), p 165.
77. A. Rossi (note 71), p 9. For what follows see also J.W. Brügel, *Stalin und Hitler. Pakt gegen Europa*, Vienna 1973, especially pp 96 ff, and A. Hillgruber and K. Hildebrand, *Kalkül zwischen Macht und Ideologie. Der Hitler–Stalin Pakt: Parallelen bis heute?*, Zurich 1980.
78. A. Rossi (note 71) p 37.
79. Quoted from *Keesing's Contemporary Archives*, 31 October 1939, p 4297.
80. A. Rossi (note 71), p 63.
81. Ibid, p 165.
82. Ibid, p 141.
83. Ibid, p 215.
84. P. Leverkuehn, *Der geheime Nachrichtendienst der deutschen Wehrmacht im Kriege*, Frankfurt 1957, p 82.
85. Ibid, p 83.
86. W. von Schramm, *. . . sprich vom Frieden, wenn du den Krieg willst*, Mainz 1973. New edition with the title *Hitler und die Franzosen*, Mainz 1980.
87. A. Rossi, *Zwei Jahre deutsch-sowjetisches Bündnis*, Cologne/Berlin 1954, pp 102 ff.
88. D. Hyde, *Anders als ich glaubte*, Freiburg 1953, p 92.
89. A. Rossi (note 87), p 282.
90. A. Rossi (note 71), p 282.
91. Ibid, pp 327 ff.

92. Ibid, p 122.

93. E. Topitsch, *Die Sozialphilosophie Hegels als Heilslehre und Herrschaftsideologie*, second edition, Munich 1981.

94. K. Marx and F. Engels, *Werke*, vol. 29, Berlin 1963, pp 160 ff.

95. J. Wuescht, *Jugoslawien und das Dritte reich*, Stuttgart 1969, p 173. Stalin sometimes made use of the Russian Orthodox Church for his political propaganda, especially when he was trumpeting the great peace offensive of the late forties and fifties: see J.S. Curtiss, *Die Kirche in der Sowjetunion 1917–1956*, Munich 1957, pp 287 ff, especially 298 ff.

96. S. Allard (note 53), p 42.

97. Ibid, p 43.

98. Ph. W. Fabry (note 66), p 412.

99. H. Pächter (note 39), p 128.

100. Ph. W. Fabry (note 66), p 290. The second quote comes from S. Myllyniemi, *Die baltische Krise 1938–1941*, Stuttgart 1979, pp 118, 126.

101. Ph. W. Fabry, *Der Hitler–Stalin Pakt 1939–1941*, Darmstadt 1962, p 212.

102. Ibid, p 243.

103. B. S. Telpuchowski, *Die sowjetische Geschichte des Grossen Vaterländischen Krieges 1941–1945*, edited and with notes by A. Hillgruber and H.A. Jacobsen, Frankfurt 1961, p 32.

104. Ph. W. Fabry (note 101), p 260.

105. Ibid.

106. Ibid, p 270. As early as the summer of 1940 the Soviet General Staff made plans for a conflict with Germany, submitting them to Stalin in September 1940: see A. M. Vassilevski, *Sache des ganzen Lebens*, Berlin 1977, pp 90 ff.

107. K. Marx and F. Engels, *Werke*, vol. 2, Berlin 1959, p 543.

108. B. S. Telpuchowski (note 103), pp 30 ff.

109. *Geschichte des Grossen Vaterländischen Krieges der Sowjetunion*, vol. 1, Berlin 1962, p 514.

110. Ibid. (Italics in original.) This portrayal and analysis of Soviet military doctrine, organisation and armaments policy has now been completed and confirmed in its essential points by J.F. Hoffmann's copious researches in the volumes produced by H. Boog and others, *Der Angriff auf die Sowjetunion* (vol. 4, *Das Deutsche Reich und der Zweite Weltkrieg*), Stuttgart 1983.

111. Ibid, pp 516 ff.

112. E. Helmdach, *Täuschungen und Versäumnisse. Kriegsausbruch 1939–1941*, Berg a. See 1979, pp 91 ff.

113. S. Bialer (ed.), *Stalin and His Generals*, New York 1969, p 151. Schukov gives another description according to which 'there were many dramatic moments for the east, the "red" side; these in many ways anticipated what happened after 22 June 1941, when Germany attacked the Soviet Union.' Later the marshal, who was the leader of the 'blue' attackers, stated that he had urged that the fortification lines in the central section should be put back. This statement is perhaps designed to relieve himself of his share of the blame for the debacle of the summer of 1941 – he was at the time Chief of the General Staff. However, it may have been a genuine attempt made by a competent military leader to point out that the actual condition of the Red Army was far from adequate for the ambitious military theories being bandied about and that time was needed for modernisation in armaments and general re-organisation.

114. E. Helmdach (note 112) and A. M. Vassilevski (note 106), p 100 (quote on p 102).

115. I. C. Bagramjan, *So begann der Kreig*, Berlin 1972, p 167.

116. Ph. W. Fabry (note 66), pp 312 ff.

117. P. Gosztony, *Die Rote Armee*, Vienna/Munich/Zurich/New York 1980, p 194. Quote from B. Pietrov, *Stalinismus, Sicherheit, Offensive. Das 'Dritte Reich' in der Konzeption der sowjetschen Aussenpolitik 1933-1941*, Melsungen 1983, pp 276 ff.

118. A. Werth, *Russland im Kreig 1941-1945*, Munich/Zurich 1965, p 115.
119. *Geschichte . . .* (note 109), vol. I, p 563.
120. Ibid, p 508.
121. A. M. Vassilevski (note 106), p 100. The doctrine of the 'easy war' was not without its opponents. For example, it was criticised in the spring of 1940 by the Central Committee, perhaps owing to the experience of the Finnish War (Ibid, p 96). Possibly there was also some concern that too much self-confidence might prejudice efforts in the armaments industry and also in the military sphere. See M. Morozov, *Die Falken des Kreml*, Munich 1982, p 238, 240 ff.
122. Hillgruber and Jacobsen (note 103) give a summary of the very considerable aid offered, p 572.
123. Details based on German Army High Command documents, according to Hillgruber and Jacobsen (note 103), p 41.
124. E. Helmdach (note 112), p 61. Somewhat different figures from A. Seaton, *Der russisch–deutsche Kreig 1941–1945*, Frankfurt 1973, p 104 – namely, 600,000 prisoners and more than 5,000 destroyed or captured tanks.
125. A. Werth (note 118), p 288.
126. J. Erickson (note 10), p 99.
127. *Geschichte . . .* (note 109), vol. I, p 485 ff.
128. G. K. Schukov (note 5), p 196.
129. Ibid, p 197.
130. Ph. W. Fabry (note 66), p 354, Cf P. Grigorenko, *Der sowjetische Zusammenbruch 1941*, Frankfurt 1969, p 27: 'In reality the German tanks were not superior even to our older models (T-26, BT-5 and BT-7).'
131. A. Seaton (note 124), p 74.
132. G. K. Schukov (note 5), p 197. J. Hoffmann (note 110), p 75, even comes to this conclusion: 'The superiority of the armed forces of the Soviet Union in tanks, artillery and aircraft over the German army, now in a two-front war, seems absolutely enormous if one takes into consideration the total number of available weapons and war materials . . . Soviet industry has reached a stage and created all the conditions to provide very quickly an absolutely stupendous supply of armaments.'
133. E. Helmdach, *Uberfall?*, fourth edition, Neckargemund 1978, p 32.
134. A. Hillgruber (note 9), pp 207 ff.
135. F. H. Hinsley, *Hitlers Strategie*, Stuttgart 1952, p 188.
136. F. Halder, *Kreigstagebuch*, vol. 1, Stuttgart 1962–1964, p 375.
137. A. Hillgruber (note 9), pp 218 ff.
138. F. Halder (note 136), vol 2, pp 31 ff.
139. Ph. W. Fabry (note 101), p 297.
140. G. Gafencu (note 4), pp 96 ff.
141. Ibid, pp 107 ff.
142. Ibid, p 110.
143. Ph. W. Fabry (note 101), p 316.
144. Ibid, p 324.
145. A. Hillgruber (note 9), p 222.
146. *Geschichte . . .* (note 109). pp 464 ff.
147. L. Besymenski, *Sonderakte Barbarossa*, Reinbek bei Hamburg 1973, p 157.
148. V. Bereshkov, *In diplomatischer Mission bei Hitler in Berlin 1940–41*, Frankfurt 1967, pp 23 ff. Actually Bereshkov was not present at the discussions with Hitler, as is shown by the list of participants. See Ph. W. Fabry (note 66), p 455, note 50.
149. A. Hillgruber (note 9), p 306, note 17 (from W. Leonard, *Die Zeit*, 7 May 1965).
150. A. Seidl (note 67), pp 229 ff. *Die Aufzeichnungen uber die Gesprache folgen*, p 245 ff.
151. A. Seidl (note 67), p 268.
152. Ibid, p 286.

153. P. Schmidt (note 54), p 517.
154. Ibid, p 521.
155. Ibid.
156. A. Seidl (note 67), p 266.
157. Ibid, pp 283 ff. V. Bereshkov (note 148), p 29, reports: 'A telegram from Moscow caused Molotov to adopt a much harder attitude on the second day of the negotiations. The ominous disclosures in the air-raid shelter were therefore obviously the result of a direct order from Stalin.'
158. Ph. W. Fabry (note 66), pp 256 ff.
159. A. Seidl (note 67), p 192.
160. G. Gafencu (note 4), p 150.
161. J. Byrnes, *Speaking Frankly*, New York/London 1947, p 288.
162. D. Irving, *Hitler und seine Feldherren*, Frankfurt/Berlin/Vienna 1975, p 184. E. Hughes, *Churchill – Ein Mann in Widerspruch*, Tübingen 1959, p 182. Recently B. Pietrov (note 117) remarks that Molotov's self-confident attitude was 'a challenge for the host', but neither author makes any further deductions from their observations.
163. *Geschichte . . .* (note 109), vol. 2, p 32. D. Hyde (note 88), pp 126 ff, for example, describes how those sympathy campaigns were organised.
164. G. Gafencu (note 4), p 172.
165. Quote from Gafencu (note 4), p 174.
166. Ibid, p 199. M. Morozov (note 121), pp 240 ff, 245.
167. A. Seidl (note 67), p 372.
168. H. Lupke, *Japans Russlandpolitik von 1939 bis 1941*, Frankfurt 1962, pp 99 ff, 110 ff. G. Gafencu (note 4), p 208: 'Moscow demanded that the value of the new agreement was to be absolute, not relative, and that it assured Japan's neutrality towards the Soviet Union even in the event of a German–Russian war, just as it gave Japan a guarantee of Russia's neutrality if there was a conflict in the Pacific.'
169. H. Lupke (note 168), p 126, note 170.
170. Ibid, p 130.
171. G. Gafencu (note 4), p 209. Such intentions had not remained unnoticed by the Americans – see F. Knipping (note 52), p 26: 'There were worries in the State Department that Russia would exploit American attempts at a rapprochement only to bring about the assumed irrevocable Soviet goal in its Far East policy, which was to bring nearer a war between Japan and the U.S.A.' Laurence A. Steinhardt, U.S. Ambassador in Moscow from 1939 to 1941 'believed that the Soviet government considered a non-aggression pact with Japan as a lever to unleash a war in the Pacific, which had always been the aim of Soviet foreign policy. They knew in Moscow that Japan could only lose such a war and that the fruits of a Japanese collapse . . . would in the end fall automatically into the lap of the Soviet Union, the strongest power in the Far East' (op. cit. p 165). But Roosevelt's foreign policy often ignored the State Department and in 1941 Steinhardt was relieved of his office. Incidentally there was a Russo–Japanese pact directed against the U.S.A. as early as 1916 – see B. Martin, *Friedensinitiativen und Machtpolitik in Zweiten Weltkrieg 1939–1942*, Dusseldorf 1976, p 17.
172. *Geschichte . . .* (note 109), vol. 1, pp 467 ff.
173. Ph. W. Fabry (note 101), pp 379 ff.
174. A. Werth (note 118), p 102.
175. Ph. W. Fabry (note 66), pp 288 ff.
176. G. K. Schukov (note 5), pp 288 ff.
177. Ph. W. Fabry (note 101), pp 279 ff. A Seidl (note 67), pp 409 ff.
178. W. S. Churchill (note 42), III/1, Berne 1950, p 421.
179. A. Werth (note 118), p 104.
180. J. W. Brugel (note 77), p 232.
181. Ph. W. Fabry (note 66), pp 413 ff.

147

182. J. W. Brugel (note 77), pp 290 ff.

183. Ph. W. Fabry (note 66), pp 308, 337, 365 ff.

184. Ibid, p 362.

185. J. Wuescht (note 95), p 175, even has reports of documents which were said to have fallen into the hands of a German assault party in the Soviet Embassy building in Belgrade, which the Soviets had had to leave hastily. One of the documents is said to have stated: "The U.S.S.R. will only react when the time is ripe. The Axis powers have squandered most of their forces and therefore the Soviet Union will suddenly attack Germany . . .' But Wuescht's sources are inaccurate and B. Pietrov (note 117), p 316, objects that 'there was no evidence of what kind of a document it was or where it was found'.

186. A. Werth (note 118), p 106.

187. Ibid, p 107.

188. G. Hilger (note 31), pp 307 ff, cf G. Gafencu (note 4), pp 259 ff: 'On 5 May, in a private circle of officer cadets . . . Stalin had praised the heroism of the Russian Army and declared that the soldiers of the Soviet Union must not keep to the defensive, but must be ready to show their attack capabilities in order to oppose the powers which are seeking world dominion.' J. Hoffmann (note 110), pp 73 ff, gave a very similar interpretation of Stalin's speech. Also important in this connection is the statement, quoted there, of Major-General Meandrov, later head of the Officer Training School of the Red Army, before his repatriation in 1946: 'The policy of the government to get ready for a great war was perfectly clear to us . . . what was put to us as defence measures turned out to be a long prepared and carefully disguised plan of aggression.'

189. G. Hilger (note 31), p 308.

190. G. Gafencu (note 4), p 255. At this time of direct war preparation – only thirteen days before the German attack – Dmitri Ustinov took charge of the Ministry of Armaments. He was then, at thirty-three, Stalin's youngest minister. He was later Defence Minister, a post he held till his death in 1984. This is an example of the continuity between the Stalin era and the present. See M. Morozov (note 121), p 247.

191. A. Seaton (note 124), pp 59 ff.

192. B. G. Premier gives a realistic description of these reconnaissance flights in *Der Flug zum Don*, Leoni 1981.

193. Ph. W. Fabry (note 101), pp 389 ff.

194. A. Hillgruber (note 9), p 371.

195. D. Irving (note 162), p 266.

196. F. Halder (note 34), p 34, confirms this: 'The decision to attack Russia was a very difficult one for Hitler. He was concerned about the warnings of his military advisers; the shadow of Napoleon, with whom he like to compare himself, lay over the mysterious expanses of this vast country. On the other hand, he was firmly convinced, not without reason, that Russia was preparing for an attack on Germany. *We know today from good sources that he was right in this.*' (Italics in original.)

197. Ph. W. Fabry (note 66), p 386.

198. Ibid.

199. F. Halder (note 136), vol. 2, p 353.

200. P. Gosztony (note 117), p 196. Cf also A. M. Vassilevski (note 106), p 96: 'While a number of the military leaders wanted to position the main supplies to the east, other opposed this categorically, especially Kulik Mechlis and Stschadenko, who thought the aggression would be quickly repulsed and in any case the war would be continued on enemy territory.'

201. P. Grigorenko (note 121), p 91; on the other hand, G. K. Schukov (note 5), p 210.

202. The role of such bulges, which often gives clues about intended moves, needs a closer examination. Congress Poland was such a bulge, at the time pushed out far into the west; in the Second World War there was the bulge of Kursk in 1943, and the out-curving of Thuringia towards the central Rhine; more recently there is Afghanistan, directed tow-

ards the Indian Ocean. Admittedly such manifestations are not confined to the Soviet Union: before the First World War there was the so-called 'Caprivi Finger' of German south-west Africa which pointed to the Zambesi, or, in the Cameroons, the Duck's Bill' to the Chari and the 'Lobster Claw' to the Congo.

203. Ph. W. Fabry (note 101), pp 421 ff. F. Helmdach (note 112), pp 51 ff. Ibid (note 133), pp 34 ff.
204. H. G. Seraphim, *Die deutsch–russichen Beziehungen 1939–1941*, Hamburg 1949, pp 66 ff.
205. G.K. Schukov (note 5), p 248.
206. P. Grigorenko (note 121), p 94.
207. I. C. Bagramjan (note 115), p 125.
208. Ibid, p 51.
209. Ibid, p 150. Regarding the dogma of the 'easy victory' see also P. Grigorenko (note 121), p 31.
210. I. C. Bagramjan (note 115), pp 66 ff.
211. Ibid, p 67.
212. Ibid, p 75.
213. Ibid, pp 76 ff.
214. G. K. Schukov (note 5), p 210.
215. Ph. W. Fabry (note 66), p 357.
216. G. K. Schukov (note 5), p 246.
217. E. von Manstein: *Verlorene Siege*, Bonn 1955, pp 179 ff.
218. Ph. W. Fabry (note 66), pp 363 ff.
219. G. K. Schukov (note 5), p 237.
220. I. C. Bagramjan (note 115), p 113.
221. E. Helmdach (note 112), p 58; ibid (note 133), p 35.
222. Ibid (note 112), pp 51 ff.
223. Ibid (note 133), p 56.
224. Ibid, pp 56 ff.
225. Ibid, p 58.
226. G. K. Schukov (note 5), p 237.
227. Ibid, p 229.
228. Ibid, p 231.
229. F. Halder (note 136), vol. 3, p 38.
230. G. Hilger (note 31), pp 233 ff.
231. W. von Schramm, *Geheimdienst im Zweiten Weltkrieg*, fourth edition, Munich 1983, pp 180 ff.
232. W. S. Churchill (note 42), III/1, p 440.
233. Ibid, p 441.
234. Ibid, p 443.
235. Ibid, p 444.
236. Ibid, III/2, p 14.
237. Ibid, III/1, pp 426 ff.
238. Ibid, III/2, p 15.
239. A. Rossi (note 87), p 479.
240. G. F. Kennan (note 18), p 479.
241. W. S. Churchill (note 42), III/2, pp 117 ff.
242. Ibid, pp 114 ff.
243. 'British Perceptions of Soviet Military Capability 1935–39', in Mommsen and Kettenacker (note 45), pp 297 ff.
244. W. S. Churchill (note 42), III/2, p 368.
245. E. von Manstein (note 217), p 156.
246. H. Feis, *The Road to Pearl Harbour*, Princeton 1950. P. Oswald, *Japans Weg von Genf*

nach San Franzisko, Stuttgart 1955, pp 71 ff. M. Libal, *Japans Weg in den Kreig*, Dusseldorf 1971.

247. A. Hillgruber (note 6), p 76.

248. C. von Clausewitz, *Vom Kriege*, Book VIII, Chapter 9 (edition of W. Hahlweg, Bonn 1952, pp 922 ff).

249. W. S. Churchill (note 42) VI/1, p 168.

250. H. Feis, *Churchill–Roosevelt–Stalin*, Princeton 1957, p 275.

251. R. E. Sherwood, *Roosevelt und Hopkins*, Hamburg 1948, p 612. (Italics in original.)

252. W. S. Churchill (note 42), VI/1, p 168.

253. H. Feis, (note 250), p 596.

254. G. F. Kennan (note 18), p 475. An impressive assessment of the leading Americans' political intelligence at the time is given by R. E. Sherwood (note 251), pp 212 ff, who reports what Harry Hopkins later told him of the conference at Yalta: 'In our hearts we really believed a new day had dawned, the day we had for so many years longed for and about which we had talked so much. We were all convinced we had won the first great victory for peace, and when I say we, I mean all of us, all civilised mankind. The Russians had proved that they could be reasonable and farsighted and neither the President nor any one of us had the slightest doubt that we could live with them and get on peacably with them far into the future. I must, however, make one reservation – I believe that in our hearts we made the proviso that we couldn't foretell how things would turn out if something happened to Stalin.'

255. This mistrust was revealed shortly before the end of the war, when the SS General Karl Wolff established contact in Switzerland with Alan Dulles, Head of the American Secret Service, in order to prepare for the capitulation of the German Forces in Italy. Although Moscow was informed about these contacts, they were alarmed and suspected that at the last moment the always dreaded arrangement between the Germans and the British and Americans would take place. See W. S. Churchill (note 42), VI/2, pp 116 ff.

256. H. Feis (note 250), p 361.

257. P. Kleist, *Zwischen Hitler und Stalin 1939–1945*, Bonn 1950, pp 230 ff. These happenings are very obscure and have not been satisfactorily clarified: cf A. Hillgruber, *Sowjetische Aussenpolitik im Zweiten Weltkreig*, Konigstein/Dusseldorf 1979, p 83. The German leadership rightly interpreted the Soviet initiative as an extortion manoeuvre against the Western Allies. See P. Kleist, (op. cit.), pp 273 ff.

258. These connections have proved enigmatic to many people. Some suspicion falls on the Reichsleiter, Martin Bormann. See W. von Schramm (note 231), p 226, and also H. M. Beer, *Moskaus As im Kampf der Geheimdienste: Martin Bormanns Rolle in der Fuhrungsspitze des Dritten Reiches*, second edition, Paehr/Obb 1984.

259. A. Seaton (note 124), pp 460 ff.

260. W. S. Churchill (note 42), p 235.

261. On these events see M. Boveri, *Der Verrat im 20 Jahrhundert IV*, Reinbek 1960.

261. M. Weber, *Wirtschaft und Gesellschaft*, fourth edition, Tübingen 1956, p 13.

262. Ibid, p 29.

263. C. von Clausewitz (note 248), pp 89 ff.

264. H. Rauschning, *Gespräche mit Hitler*, Vienna/Zurich/New York 1947, pp 74 ff.

265. See note 254.

266. M. Boveri (note 261), p 63.

267. V. Suvorov, 'Who was planning to attack whom in June 1941 – Hitler or Stalin?', *Journal of the Royal United Services Institute for Defence Studies*, June 1985, pp 60 ff. 'Yes, Stalin was planning to attack Hitler in June 1941', ibid, June 1986, pp 73 ff.

268. Ibid, June 1985, p 54.

Index

The names of Hitler and Stalin are not listed as they occur throughout the text.